TALES OF THE CONFLENT

A GLYMPSE OF PARADYSE

A PYRENNEAN PARADISE RELATED THROUGH
TALES ABOUT THOSE WHO LIVE THERE

Volume 1 : First Impressions

Contents

The Prologue to the Conflent Tales

The drofte of Merche's root has been truly perced and April is dripping with soote shoures. Another journey has begun. Those of you who haven't sampled the delights of Chaucer's Prologue to the Canterbury Tales whilst dozing in the back row of a hot schoolroom may be wondering whether you have picked the right language. In that case start here! That was just a bit of show. So here beginneth a new and different prologue. For Canterbury read Conflent – that's not a bad swap. For Chaucer read Longworth – well, you can't have it all! Hold on a tick. The Conflent – where's that? Nowhere near Canterbury, that's for sure. It's about a thousand miles further South and in a different country. So will this travel book last 700 years like the first one? Who knows, but the odds are that it will be as durable as the thousand year Reich was. There's one thing in its favour – it isn't your standard travel guide. They're so dull. Go here, go there, see this, see that, stay in this hotel, avoid that restaurant. Nothing about what makes a region tick. Nothing about the people, except occasionally the historical toffs who were born there, and they're usually dead. Nothing to give the reader insights into the manners, mores, habits, lives, loves, pain and laughter that gives the true story of a real place where real people live. Nothing to unlock the door to the secret garden of a region and lay bare its true soul. Until now! And so, it is with such an excruciating mixed metaphor that we unfold the Conflent Tales.

In effect, this is a travel book, a set of adventure stories and a confessional all rolled into one, and brought to the reader through the mouths of those who live in this hidden paradise. One author, many mouths. And beware! It's funny. Gosh it's funny! Subtly, rhetorically and guffawly funny. When the opening caste of the book first purchased their Conflent farmhouse in 1989, they were not expecting to make it a permanent residence. At that time they were returning to England from a six year stretch in Paris and Brussels, and both work obligations and the other intrusive commitments of two busy lives seemed to stretch a long way into the future. Professing and Nursing were the thieves of all their time. The opportunity to think about anything more than a week ahead was a rare luxury. But fortune's finger and idle circumstance around 1992 combined to make such a move a possibility, and after a long and introspective reflection, that possibility was transformed into fact a year later. The journey into the paradise of the Conflent had begun. From being a place to visit two or three times a year to become immersed in paint tins, garden cuttings and mortar, the *mas* des Oliviers became the centre of the universe - a huge 3-storey dog kennel for Artur into which he gladly invited us, if only to open the tins of pedigree pal. And a reason to write these tales of the heart of a region through its actors.

It is said, with some trepidation by those who would rather keep the secret, that the Conflent will be the next region of France to attract the foreign invader, the Dordogne, Riviera and Provence having become too expensive. The *franc fort*, which made the pound look like monopoly money in the mid-nineties, was first superceded by the *livre fort*, in which Brits in their thousands searched for a place to call their own in foreign fields.

More recently the *euro fort,* after fluctuating like a Greek tax break, joined the eurozone slide into oblivion, and the pound/euro exchange rate once more favoured the brits. Only the most prescient of soothsayers can predict what will happen in the future, but the new situation hasn't yet reanimated the invasion of *l'Albion perfide'* to these elysian pastures. The credit crunch and its aftermath didn't help of course. House prices slid downwards in inverse ratio to bankers' bonuses. It's still in a deep depression that neither whisky nor hypnotherapy can halt. But it will return. The

Conflent has all the advantages of climate, mountain environment, relative cheapness of property and a people desperate to experience the wonders of cricket.

It is as far as one can get from England and still be in France, with the splendours of Spain close by. Where else can one pluck a luscious ripe peach while looking out at a 9000 foot snow-capped mountain, typing a book out on a sunny balcony surrounded by rolling hills and verdant valleys, with a babbling brook flowing by and the nightingales just tuning up for their evening symphony - as I am doing at the present moment. If there is a mosquito within two miles, the local entomological society will want to know about it. Equally the Coronavirus – not enough people to bother them. Better pickings in the cities.

But all paradises also have a dark side. Despite, perhaps because of, its great beauty, the Conflent is a region of high unemployment and barely hidden poverty. So these tales have another purpose and that is to bring in greater wealth from tourism. Anyone who reads them and doesn't want, nay yearn, to visit the Conflent might consider donating their heart for use at the Eus boulodrome.
Hidden in the midst of the light-heartedness and laughter there is a more important message. Readers who get as far as the last chapter of volume two receive not only the biscuit but an insight into why it was written. And yet, in the last twenty years our intrepid travellers have met so many wonderful people, heard so many marvellous stories and survived so many blissful experiences that our heroes couldn't keep the secret any longer. They had to tell it and so did their animals and the people for whom the Conflent is ingrained in their bones. Others might hate them for blowing the gaff, but here, in the Conflent, is the journey into paradise, related through the lives of the people who found and founded it.
Norman Longworth , Eus, France

About the Author

Norman Longworth is a former professor who has published many boring academic books and papers that sell slowly to other boring academics around the world. He has a world-wide reputation for setting up lifelong learning cities and you can't get more boring than that. However in his self-published books there is another Norman Longworth – one set free from the chains of academia and who sees publishing as a playground for using words creatively and telling stories. He also writes deathless poetry and eyewatering music to the poems. His prose books so far are travel books with a difference but he intends to branch out with a wide variety of other poetry forms, including the doggerel verse of 'lancashire monologues' - an artform that flourished in his native region in the late 19th and early 20th century. When not professing or writing he golfs badly, and plays the piano excruciatingly in his South of France home. He can be contacted through his website www.longlearn.info

Since the Conflent, which, admit it, you have never heard of, is one of the most beautiful regions on earth, let's start with a poem. But don't worry. This is not a poetry book. There are a few within its pages and you have every right to ignore them if you so wish. Anyway here goes.

<u>The Sublime Conflent</u>

Land of high mountains, land blessed by sun
Land of deep valleys where wild creatures run
Land of antiquity, smooth age-worn stone
Land of wild beauty, nature's royal throne

Land where the eagles heavenwards soar
Land of the hiker, the hunter, the boar
Land of migration the avian fleet
Seeking escape to the sun's radiant heat

Land of great moment where time's tranquil crawl
Reveals its rich past on each weathered wall
Land of fine churches with rare baroque treasure
Soaking man's senses in cerebral pleasure

Land of great music in abbey and hall
Where once Pau Casals played his cello to all
Land of grand festivals every saint's day
Where villagers party the sweet night away

Land of the river, the Tet's brimming breast
Inspires nature's bounty to feed the distressed
Land of high pastures, of long transhumance
Land that will captivate, charm and entrance

Land of fair Eus, a village of art
An exquisite vision that quickens the heart
Perched on its hillside, a precious bijou
Each building seeking a Canigou view

Land of the Canigou, mountain sublime
Sacred in Catalan folklore through time
Regal. Majestic, compelling all
Its subjects below to live in its thrall

Land of bold Vernet where Kipling once strode
There where the hot healing waters still flowed
Land of old Villefranche, Vauban's true delight
Now a UNESCO World Heritage site

This is the Conflent a true paradise
A land with a value beyond any price
Land of great beauty where magic doth roam
This is the Conflent - that now is our home
©Norman Longworth

TALES OF THE CONFLENT

CHAPTER THE FYRST

THE YMMYGRANT'S TALE

Or

Paradyse Found

The Conflent Tales

The Ymmygrants Tale

We came, Maggie, Artur and me in the sweltering May of 1993. There is a fork in the *Autoroute du Soleil* at Avignon. The saying goes that those who are rich turn left to the Riviera and those without much worldly wealth turn right towards Nîmes and Montpellier. Those who are almost destitute finally make it to Perpignan and the *département* of the *Pyrénées-Orientales* where macho Spain kisses la belle France on her southernmost border. A few more kilometres to the west-south-west of the city and there, where the mountains shake hands with the plain, is the location of the Conflent, one of the best-kept secrets of France.

I came from England, born and bred as a northern barbarian, softened by the mellow living of the Southern Counties, and culturally matured by the experience of six years breathing in the elegant fumes of Paris and Brussels. Three years previously, I had eagerly returned with my wife to our native land, hoping to take up life in our small Hampshire town where we had left it six years previously. But this was not to be. The fault perhaps lay in ourselves. During our years abroad we had changed and England had changed. But we seemed to have changed in opposite directions, and this produced an incompatibility with our own heritage which we could not shake off.

We had both become that tabloid figure of revulsion, European, more open to other cultures and languages, more tolerant of people and customs, more understanding of non British habits and values, excited by the dream of a co-operating Europe free of conflict for the first time in thousands of years, able to compete on equal terms with other global super-powers. The Britain of the time appeared to us to have lost the outward-looking idealism which made it such a special place to live, and we found ourselves out of step with utilitarian governance, xenophobia and tabloid power and values.

I love my country, but as the new soft white underbelly of a nation where holding wider and different international ideals seemed to have become a dubious, if not criminal, practice, we both had to leave once more. The ugly weather of that year, too, had a part to play, having produced a mental gout difficult to throw off.

During the years abroad we had voyaged throughout Europe and the world, courtesy of IBM, as if travelling would soon go out of fashion. Frequently Artur would accompany us on our excursions to every part of the continent. It seemed to be preferable to putting him in kennels, though we often had to do this too. Artur, as you may have guessed, is what you would call a dog, but what we would call a member of the family - a Briard or Berger de Brie, born in Normandy but ancestrally bred to impose his will on the sheep in the region South East of Paris. I suppose that would make him a *chien*, rather than a dog, but although he is a bi-lingual animal, the more esoteric nuances of semiology seem to escape him. To us he is an intelligent, diverting and amusing companion, if a little bewildered by our constant changes of habitat.

My wife and I spend many an hour laughing at Artur's jokes and he, for his part, at ours.
Often he is the only one who appreciates them. Maggie speaks to him as if he were a human being, admittedly one with a limited vocabulary, but nevertheless he seems to understand everything She says

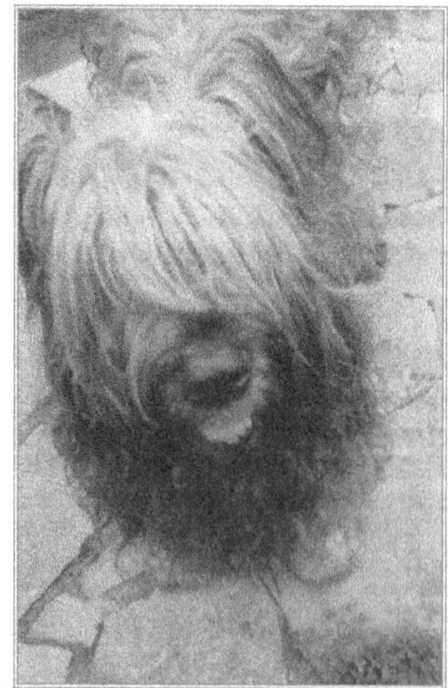

When we are forced to leave him behind on a shopping expedition, she would tell me that she had explained to Artur why he had to stay at home and what he had to do while we were out. I sometimes wonder about Maggie's ability to understand me (it works both ways), but I never have any doubt about Artur's ability to understand Maggie, nor she him.

But why here? The Conflent? Paradise regained? In 1990, just before our return, we had spent some days with friends in Port Barcarès on the Mediterranean coast near to where the Pyrennees yield to the sea. The *stations balnéaires*, seaside resorts, here might be described as brave new contemporary, concrete and crépi architectural egg cartons built in a hurry as a result of massive subventions from the state and from the European Commission in order to create new jobs in an area of high unemployment.

They took advantage of an unspoilt 80 mile long stretch of sandy beach from the Spanish border to the *étang de Leucate*, a sheltered sea-water lake separated from the Mediterranean Sea by a narrow spit of land. For those who like sea, sand, sun and wind-surfing this coastline is a paradise. The sun burns down for more than 300 days in the year, the sand is castle-friendly and soft at the same time, and the wind descends from the mountains with frequent regularity. Its only drawback is that the ferocity of the *tramontane*, the local equivalent of the *mistral*, can sometimes blow people off the beach and send the wind surfers speeding off at 100 miles an hour towards the African coast.

To continue. Whilst in the Belgian twentieth century concrete bunker city, we had contacted an estate agent with English-speaking staff, there for the sole purpose of seducing such vulnerable and impressionable Brits as we were at the time. During our spell in Paris we had explored every inch of France and fallen madly in love with the country. So France was where we decided to lay down our aging bones and impose our rudimentary language skills on the natives. But where? The obvious answer is as far as we could get from the UK and still be in France.

So late October 1989 found us near the med, spending a thoroughly blissful couple of weeks researching the whole area of the *Pyrenées Orientales* and the *Corbières* for potential permanent accommodation wherein to lay down new roots.

We can thoroughly recommend this as a geographical and cultural pastime. How else can one afford the services of a free daily guide to the sights of the local region, inspect the habitat and ways of life of the local bipedal fauna, and be frequently entertained to meals? It's a much under-rated activity and it's free. Even if the dream-house hits you in the eyes on the first day, better to feign continuing interest in order to continue the whole pampering experience. In a rustic region like this one, rarely does your first choice go quickly.

Our excursions into the stunning hinterland took us into well-preserved mediaeval towns, narrow limestone defiles and gorges, singular outcrops and splendid mountain-top views and some of the most precarious and picturesque roads on the face of this earth. Villages perched perilously over thousand foot drops, sunlit hamlets on bare hill-tops, settlements hidden in deep chasms.

We saw houses large and small, mansions town and country, *maisons de maître* and *de village*, fortified *bastides,* poky habitations built into town ramparts, and secluded dwellings miles from the nearest loo let alone electricity, gas and water. Life here must have been one long search for urgent relief. We observed buildings without walls, studied residences without roofs, researched barns without doors and occasionally examined edifices with all those missing parts.

One house in the village of *Davejean* in the *Corbière* mountains was blessed with eight bedrooms, an enormous kitchen and living room - and those were just on the first two floors. Two more undeveloped floors rose above this, capped by a massive terrace which opened up a superb view over the surrounding limestone countryside. The estate agent apologised for the outrageous price - £9,000 - but pointed out that we could probably knock the owners down since it needed some money spent on it. Indeed it did. It was a veritable bank-buster, though an even greater drawback was the remoteness of its situation in a small hamlet 45 kilometres from the next habitation. For a family of 17 attracted to the idea of eternal solitude, delighting in its own company and prepared for a mountain of DIY it would have been perfect. For our more sociable spirits it held little attraction,

Eventually however we were to be seduced by the house we now live in, a perfect *mas* in a perfect setting. But more of that story later. That's one for my wife. Our home is in the Conflent and at the risk of turning this so early into a Geography lesson – not everyone shares my passion for understanding the natural landscape where they live, but it won't take long, I promise you - I will try to be more specific.

All around the regional capital, Perpignan, almost into Spain, is found one of the most fertile areas of France, the small triangular plain of the Roussillon, home to the wines of that name and to one of the largest fruit-growing regions of France. Home also to two of the most intoxicating of aperitif wines, the *Muscat de Rivesaltes* and the *vin de Banyuls*, natural *vins doux* consumed in copious abandon by most of the population of the plain.

Three rivers flow into the plain from the Pyrennees and their foothills. I won't call them mighty - even in England they would be classed as little more than flowing puddles and in summer they tend to dry up completely - but over the aeons they have helped to grind down the solid rock of the mountains, transforming it into fertile soil and transporting it to the plain below. The middle one of these three, the Têt, is the most accessible of these, and just before it takes a reluctant leave of the hills to meander quietly over the flat land is the realm of the Conflent. It is the place where we now live and have our being.

Travelling eastwards from our home, we can traverse the sun-drenched plain and within 30 minutes confront the warm welcoming waters of the Mediterranean sea, at this point clear and clean, and not quite so likely to dissolve the human bather as it is in other more notorious and richer coastal areas. Driving westwards we can ascend the ever-narrowing cleft of the river Têt, upwards ever upwards, into the Kingdom of the *Cerdagne*, an enormous hanging valley some four thousand feet above sea level, on the flanks of which will be found some of the excellent ski slopes of the Eastern Pyrennees.

The Val d'Isère, the Oberlech Valley or the slopes of Cortina d'Ampezzo they are not, but they are enough to satisfy our simple needs to mess about on planks of plastic in the winter. Northwards lie the *Fenouillèdes* - foothills of the Pyrennees, undulating territories of upland *vignobles* and home to the *Côtes du Roussillon Villages*, which everyone in this area knows to be the best of the local wines.

These are lands of summer mystery and winter snow where lonely travellers can drive for hours without a glimpse of another vehicle, imagining that they have driven into a magic Narniac world where no other human exists, and where only the murmur of the bees, the beauty of the landscape and the droning of the engine disturbs the philosophy of the moment.

To the South, brooding, smiling, scowling, towering - presiding magisterially over earth and people alike - are the 9000 feet of the *Canigou* massif, the sacred mountain of the Catalans, and snow-capped for ten months of the year. To say that it dominates would be an understatement, an insult to the mountain. It eclipses all else and breathes its power over everything and everyone.

It could be Zeus's second home if he had a mind to leave Olympus for the summer holidays. It is an obligatory focus for the orientation of every house within its visual dominion, that they may worship it the better. It is almost as if the class system is replaced here by a 'view of Canigou' system, each house and householder straining to claim a sight of as much of the mountain as it can, even if it be only from a window in the topmost part of the chimney.

The Canigou – Sacred Mountain of the Catalans – presides magisterially over the Conflent Countryside

Maisons de Village in the narrow streets of the many peasant communities of the Conflent somehow achieve the impossible feat of a *Canigou* view, through a narrow slit in the row opposite, via a strategically placed skylight in the South facing side of the roof through which they poke their heads when needing a *Canigou* fix, or perched on a precarious terrace, access to which is through a small attic window. The aristocracy in this system is the farmers and é*trangers* like us who live in the *mas, en pleine campagne* in the middle of the valley. Here balconies are constructed to maximise the Canigou panorama, proudly venerating the mountain and striving to capture, like expert painters, the subtle changes of colour and shade taking place minute by passing minute.

So here we are, wedged luxuriously between the warm tideless sea, the snowy slopes, the abundant wine terraces and a mountain that defies description of its full majesty. But there is yet more. The *Conflent* is above all a fruit growing region. For immigrants from the industrial North that is a never-ending wonder. The soil is as rich as a retired banker.

Plant a walking stick and it will grow into a fruit tree. The land is awash with budding Newtons all with the apple bruises to show. Apricots, large, fleshy and juicy ones, abound for the picking. Nectarines, almonds, pears, sweet chestnuts, figs, kiwis and cherries speak to each other of their luck in growing in such a place. It is said that God checks out the *Conflent* before growing His own orchards to see if He can compete in quality, and then gives up trying to contend with perfection.

The peaches are the pride and joy of the valley. Peaches such as these are never seen in the Northern countries of Europe. They wouldn't last the journey. When we have British visitors in summer, their eyes become almost as big as the peaches themselves. Large, like oversized cricket balls, and with the colour of ripe cherries. One picks them from the tree and looks for the seam in order to bowl that perfect late reverse swinging yorker. Except that, in this case, they are so lusciously soft that the mind is diverted from the sweet game of cricket to the more mundane pleasures of mastication.

The teeth meet little resistance as they sink into that tender orb. We commented on this new experience to our farmer neighbours, Pierre and Ambert, who, every summer, gratuitously leave boxes of them on our window-sill until we scream for peach relief. 'Ah,' they say 'They are the '*pêches de montagne'*, they are our secret weapon.' 'No' we say 'They are *les vraies pêches Banet* and anyone who has not tasted a '*pêche Banet'* has not lived with the Gods'. They are pleased with that, being proud of their work, and it also keeps the supply route open in our direction. It is a pity that distance and distribution systems are inadequate to make these secret weapons available to the northern housewife. It is the ultimate peach experience.

Blossom time is the most magnificent. In February, March and April the whole valley is a riot of pinks, whites and pale reds. From the air it is a delicate magic carpet woven in intricate splendour by the blooming trees.

Peach blossom rules! The Prades Valley in the Conflent at Blossom time

It twists and gyrates, murmurs and whispers, with the spring winds. It reflects the turquoise sheen of the cloudless sky. It is a lush, plush resting place for any passing celestial being. It is what cherry-blossom time is to the Japanese.

We have taken endless photographs of the *Conflent* in Spring. The album groans silently each time we insert another deathless view of the peach blossom. Peach blossom against the *Canigou*, peach blossom encircling our *mas*, peach blossom gazing at the village, peach blossom superimposed on peach blossom.

March – A peach of a month

Maggie, Artur and I love to walk and drive at this season. It is as if we are traversing along, across, beneath, diagonally through, the weaves and wefts of an ethereal pink canopy grown especially for our benefit.

A land of villages

France is, above all, a land of villages, and the Conflent is no exception. We are awash with them, big, small, ramparted, open, on the flat valley, perchés on the mountain side. Each village has its own character, its own church and its own patron saint, and on our arrival, we immediately made it our business to explore them with Artur. There is Rodes - a magnificent sight from the main road backed by a ridge of sandstone, capped by an ancient castle now in ruins, and nestling - Oh how it nestles! - like a new-born kitten in the lap of its mother.

All flowers and front hedges, leading down to a village square almost inundated by plane trees, and continuing to the banks of the River Têt along which one can wander through a narrow gorge to the fruit fields beyond. The other direction leads the curious wanderer upwards, through steep tiny streets and by ancient red-roofed cottages to the inevitable church at the summit of the village, dominating, magnetic, influencing as it has done through the passing ages.

The Village of Marquixanes – white-walled, red-roofed, church-capped and the newer 20th century houses now spilling out into the surrounding plain. In the background the foothills of the Fenouilledes

Round its southern periphery are the new manifestations of modern life, the bungalows and neat gardens which offer an ostensibly higher standard of living to the younger inhabitants of the village. Typical of the pampered, mollycoddled, self-indulgent peoples of the twenty-first century, they have spurned the delights of living in Aunt Jemimah's old dark, draughty and damp village stone cottage for the doubtful pleasure of an ugly modern semi with beige rendering, slate tiles and a central heating system.

And who can blame them for doing so, though it is with some regret that the traditional dwellings of village history are allowed to crumble in decay and desolation. It is only the old, the *étrangers* and the second-homers from the towns who are now preserving many villages from ruin. Potential house buyers of less than 60 years old in the remoter villages of stunningly beautiful regions such as the *Corbières* will, as we were when house-hunting, be pursued by posses of wrinkly people, begging them to restore some life and youth to the community. Life we might have been able to offer, but youth was, as Einstein discovered, a relative concept. It happened several times to us and we still dream of those lovely and gentle people, imploring us, following in clusters like wandering souls from a Hieronymous Bosch painting, sans teeth, sans purpose, sans everything except a welcoming smile, and perhaps doomed to pass the remainder of their lives in a living architectural mortuary.

The birth of Catalonia

Here in the middle *Conflent* the villages are much livelier. We paid a visit to Ria. This is a *village perché*, clinging to the hill-side, capped by the remains of yet another castle, proudly and defiantly flying the Catalan flag, nobly displaying its claim to be *le berceau de la Catalogne,* the place where Catalonia was born. Here, the story goes, is where Wilfred the Hairy was installed by Charles the Bald, then King of France, to establish his own Kingdom.

Despite the difference in tonsure, a more complementary pair could not be imagined. Wilfred was orphaned at the age of 12 as the result of a battle won by Charles on one of his sorties into what was then the territory of Aragon. The conqueror took pity on the young foundling and transported him first back to his court in Paris and thence to the magnificent castle of his sister.

Wilfred prospered and not only because he was, by all accounts, an hairy man. He learned and excelled in all the arts of knighthood and chivalry, and, at an appropriate age he was sent out to do his derring in Flanders. Such was his reputation in joust and battle that Charles was persuaded to give him his own lands and men, and so the rather dank and draughty, newly conquered castle of Ria became his headquarters and home.

But Wilfred was made of stern stuff. He craved power and authority, though by all accounts he used it to administer fair justice and to create wealth for the people as well as himself. As time passed he conquered more and more lands to the South, defeating, in the process, the Count of Barcelona and creating the land which is now known as Catalonia. In this way Ria stakes its claim to be its cradle, though who knows how the tale became enhanced with the telling. Certainly to the Barcelonans and anyone south of the Spanish border such a tale is sacrilege. They will have none of it.

We have explored the other picturesque villages that abound in the *Conflent. Villerach* and *Clara*, snuggling up to the *Canigou*, and where every waking and sleeping moment of our friends there seems to be filled by barking dogs; *Catllar*, cascading down to the bank of the *Castellan* river as if in a permanent state of mystical inspection; *Mosset*, a fortified village in the hills whose first superb aspect, all houses, red roofs and white walls, has painters scurrying home for their brushes and easels.

Indeed the village itself is seemingly populated by nothing but painters and sculptors from all parts of Europe – Britain, Holland, Germany, Spain, Switzerland – all of them creating master and mistresspieces in their converted *ateliers.* In this rugby mad region of Southern France, Mosset's ex-Mayor played rugby for his country – the 13 players per team working class variety rather than the now more popular and posher 15 game.

The Catalan Dragons Rugby League team even plays in the English league, there being a dearth of local opposition. North English industrial bastions like St Helens, Wigan, Castleford and Wakefield Trinity have now tasted the romance of gallic sweat in the scrum. Rumour has it that they are now even flavouring meals with garlic in the restaurants there, such is the insidious and pervasive influence of international sport.

Mosset's primary school feeds children from 9 nationalities into the education mills down on the plain. This is great change from the days when the local miners of talc could observe the products of their labour on the faces and bodies of men and women all over those same parts of Europe – that is, if they ever managed to escape from the village in the first place – and there is still a *'Tour des Parfums'*- a sort of olfactory museum where tourists looking for the ultimate smell sensation can snort odours and fragrances from all parts of the globe and guess where they originated..

The village of Mosset in Autumn, an artists paradise in the valley of the Castellane

Not far from the village is the 9th century abbey whose labour-of-love restoration has been immortalised in Rosemary Bailey's book 'Life in a Postcard'

At the risk of overcooking the village bit, I'll just mention the pretty spa villages. *Vernet les Bains*, a little Britain beyond France, where Rudyard Kipling played out his last raving days dreaming backwards of a 19th century of all-conquering empire, and one of the fading stars at the centre of an ex-patriate, high society, early 20th century English community which included a goodly number of Edward VII's multiple progeny. True to the spirit of its English *passants*, it is reputed to be the only town in France with a monument celebrating the entente cordiale, the African carve-up signed between Britain and France in 1904. Which is probably one more tribute to colonial greed than there is in Britain!

Vernet also boasts one of the few true Anglican churches in France, built by a subscription organised in 1913 by the man with the fine moustache, Rudyard Kipling. It is a sad sight to behold now, roof collapsing into holes, plaster falling from the walls and electricity long gone. But the good old British bum-numbing hard-wood pews are still there and the altar has survived a century of pillaging. There is even an attempt to put it back into service. A small band of devout local enthusiasts, led by a retired, visionary and not visibly eccentric Anglican pastor from Yorkshire, is seeking, and sometimes finding, the funding to restore it to its former glory. The story of this labour of love is related in Volume 3 in the Vicar's Tale.

Moving on, in this diorama of *Conflent* villages we come to *Molitg-les-Bains*, home to imposing hotels hanging over therapeutic gorges and dispensing cures for all ailments. Their impressive *troisieme empire* sanatoriums are still operating, still curing, after 100 years of *thalassotherapeutic* activity. They are a part of the highly rated, and highly expensive, French health system and where patients go for re-education, recuperation and renovation into new identities.

Les bains occurs more than once in village names of the Conflent. *St Thomas les Bains*, just to the west, is a strange and wonderful place, well-known to the many who come from far and wide to clean out the pores once a week. Two enormous open-air Jacuzzis cool the naturally-scalding water from the inner mountain down to just below blood temperature, and human beings wallow there like contented hippopotami. The best time is in the middle of winter when the outside temperature is well below zero and a shroud of icy frost permeates the air. Skiers returning from a hard day's labour in the mountains, rather like the talc miners of Mosset, drop in to the baths on their descent of the valley to join the floundering hordes, and to ease the aches and pains of a day unsuccessfully attempting to remain vertical.

It is yet another blissful experience in a blissful setting. Many strange characters may be observed here. One Swiss gentleman comes every other weekend from Geneva to relax in the water for the whole of Saturday and Sunday, though the signs stipulate a maximum of 20 minutes. He says that it the only place in the world where he has ever gained long-term relief from his permanent arthritis - long-term being about 3 hours. Another old, very old, widower came every Wednesday to wallow for hours in intimate communion with the warm jets which spew out gleeful bubbles from the sides of the bath. Last year he suffered a massive heart attack and died in the pool, but it is said by observers that, at the moment of the meeting with his maker, he wore a beatific smile on his face.

A winter scene. The pretty village of Arboussols projects itself foursquare on the top of its mountain. in the background the snow-covered mountains of the Cerdagne

And again you can find the mountain villages, many now depopulated after years of 20th century drought, situated wherever there is more than ten square metres of reasonably flat land to graze a few cows, keep sundry pigs and grow assorted vines and vegetables. These were where the hardy souls lived. Places of great beauty and vicious winter weather. Their Romanesque, still-frescoed churches betray their great age. Like Arboussols and Marcevol, perched like pyramids on the narrow road over the hills of the *Fenouillèdes,* all bustling energy in summer when the second-homers pour out from the cities to play out their rural fantasies. And in winter, cold, solitary morgues, barely inhabited by the old, the poor and the lonely.

I have even written inspiring (to me anyway) poetry about this beautiful region. To prove it here is a modest effort about the Conflent villages which I have also set to music.

Conflent Villages

The glorious Conflent villages
What wonderful tales they proclaim
Through centuries of momentous changes
In history's tempestuous name

The wise village folk of the Conflent
All share a fierce love of earth's health
Surrounded by picturesque beauty
The primary source of their wealth

Their history is built in the churches
Where rich altar-pieces entrance
In Prades, St Pierre's structure is sumptuous
The largest retable in France

These imposing sculptures interpret
The Christian message to those
Who never learned to speak latin

Or could follow the priest's rapid prose

From Rodes to the town of Olette
Enchanting communes line the route
They offer respite to the tourist
A beer? a snack? local fruit?

One such is the village of Ria
The cradle of all Catalan lands
Where the brave Wilfred the Hairy
Ensured his domains would expand

The lake and the beach near to Vinca
Are precious as newly-mined gold
Its magnificent church in the centre
Has an organ two hundred years old

The villages hard by the Cady
The river that leads to Vernet
Are sweet as the roses of summer
Corneilla, Fillols and Casteil.

On the other side of the valley
The Castellane flows to the Tet
Meandering along its green valley
Through Catllar, Molitg and Mosset

At Catllar there's a church with a belltower
By a square where grand fetes are held
At Molitg the baths are resplendent
And the view is unparalleled

Mosset's a 'beau village de France'
Crowned by a castle on high

Where each year a top-class opera
Attracts eager crowds in July

We remember the village of Eus
It's site with the fabulous view
One of France's great villages
And facing the vast Canigou

Fuilla, Sahorre, Mantet and Py
Lead up to the Pyrennean chain
Well known as the valley of apples
And airmen escaping to Spain

The villages in the high mountains
Have a history of great deprivation
More recently people have left them
For a more prosperous location

But behind all these rural facades
Families live a life beyond price
They proclaim the sheer joy of living
In the splendour of this paradise

refrain
Strong hilltop villages, small towns on the plain
Villages of beauty and friendly domains
Mountainous hamlets where the young rivers stream
The Conflent encompasses our most treasured dreams.

It's all written to music but you don't get that as well.

But the 21st century battles here are not against the weather but
against those who would change the status quo. At Marcevol, that
badge of 20th century affluence, the remains of a golf course, now
spreads its 9 tentacles over the barren hillsides. There is nothing
wrong with golf courses – to a growing proportion even of French

people, they are a thing of beauty and challenge. Here in la France profonde however there are those for whom they are the devil's playground, a foreign growth on a pure landscape, a symbol of 'other' and of the wealth they haven't themselves got.

It is not as if this was a good golf course. On the contrary, the French marines would find it difficult as an assault course. But that is by the by. Ecologists seethe, Aquarists shudder, *Agriculteurs* simmer and planners tremble. Meanwhile those charged with reviving the economic fortunes of the countryside throw up their hands in hopeless defeat. Up the valley on the road to Clara, plans were in hand to build a state-of-the-art equestrian centre with swimming pool, hotel facilities and another 9-hole golfing monster to attract even more club-wielding, saddle-strapping foreign bodies to the Conflent. After 8 years of heated discussion that was seen off the Conflent premises and has gone the way of the golf course. Modernisation of this kind is an on-going debate which touches the ambivalent soul of the people who live in this beautiful wilderness. They want none of it and they want all the economic and employment benefits it might bring at the same time.

In the high Conflent, the old farming economy of cows and pigs has gone, the vegetable gardens and vine terraces have returned to their natural state - only the human beings survive there, gaining their livelihood from forestry, sheep or the many passing tourists. It is the vine terraces which grab the imagination the most. Achingly and laboriously constructed in times past on every accessible, and even sometimes inaccessible, piece of the mountain, arduously maintained through centuries of toil by some unknown, unsung hero of the earth - hands gnarled, centuries-old faces creased through the extremes of sun, wind and frost, thin and rickety legs transporting them at a snail's pace from terrace to terrace.

Now only the traces and faces of the rocks betray the superhuman effort these people must have made to preserve a way of life growing the vines. They must have been very poor, incredibly hard-working - and extremely thirsty. I often wonder too whether they were actually happier than we are. But speculation of that kind is as old as Plato, and from the benign vantage point of the advancing twenty-first century we'll settle for our smart-alec sophistication and creature comforts before a cruel winter's day with the hoe on the mountainside.

Conflent celebrations.

Here in the Conflent we know a thing or two about celebrating. We seem to do little else. May is the month when the South of France downs tools so that it can better prepare for a summer of active hedonism in the Midi. May-day is quickly followed by VE day by Ascension Day by *Pentecôte,* each of them a wonderful excuse to *'faire le pont'*, that is to use up the days between the actual *fête* day and *le weekend* as an extra holiday. After all, it's hardly worth going in to work for just two or three days is it?

Thus, as sweet-showering April gives way to a work-free May, the festivals begin in the Conflent villages. Each village, and there is a lavish abundance of them, has its own Saint's day festival, and those that unfortunately fall in the winter make up for it by holding festivals in the summer time too. It's a matter of honour to attract the most tourists to your celebration. These summer festivals are usually weekend long celebrations of music, eating and drinking with the odd *kermesse* and a few *petanque* competitions thrown in.

The music is loud, very loud. My God, you should hear it loud, so don't forget to bring your ear-plugs. Oh and bring the wife, mistress, parents and kids as well - they'd love it if only for the noise. Here's how it works.

For the Friday evening overture, the rock band piles its biggest and most ear-splitting ghetto-blasters one on top of the other in the village square. There until 10 pm they sit in a silent and often eerie contrast to the ancient stones of the surrounding buildings. Ten pm arrives and the silence is abruptly shattered. The band arrives, pipes in a few electronically enhanced chords by way of welcome and then launches into a frenzy of noisy motion. It stays that way until two or three o clock in the morning, while the happy but deafened villagers caper and prance like cats on hot coals. The older, and wiser, take up station *behind* the stage. One number blends into another until it seems that the actual notes are irrelevant, which of course is true. Teeny-boppers, young mums and dads, older and should-be wiser heads all hop, jig, skip and swing in a seventh heaven of ecstasy.

People communicate their basic requirements - would you like to dance with me, I badly need a drink, that sausage looks extra-ordinarily tasty - by sign language. But it is all great fun for everyone. The houses vibrate alarmingly, the food tables groan extravagantly and the local wine flows abundantly. The youngsters dance the ear-splitting night away, the middle aged try energetically to recreate their faded youth. The village wrinklies, well equipped with the wisdom of age, smile on indulgently - they are probably now understanding how they came to be so deaf. And they know only too well what village festivals can do to the body. In the distance, not only the village, but the whole valley, rocks rhythmically to the music of the festival.

Saturday morning is usually silent - not merely in contrast to what has gone before but largely because of it. The middle-aged rockers of the night before lie in their beds, every movement of their aching bodies emphasising the mentally painful realisation that confronting the passing of time demands a high toll fee. The youngsters lie in their beds because they are youngsters and that is what youngsters do, and only the wrinklies move timelessly and wordlessly about the village, grateful for the luxury of an unaccustomed silence. They can't hear a thing and the flashing lights have played havoc with their eyes, but .. well, that's part of being old, isn't it?

But that does not last very long. In the afternoon all is bustle again. It is the time of the *petanque* competition, when all the brave macho men, dressed in a variety of hats, show their prowess at throwing metal balls in the proximity of each other in the village boulodrome. The *pointeurs* project their *boules* hopefully to a position somewhere near the *cochonet* (translated, and regarded, as 'little pig'), and the *tireurs* do their best to destroy the pretty patterns they make. Everything is *serieux* – the loss of an end is a *catastrophe* or a *désastre*, the winning of it a *triomphe*. French male pride is at stake and the prize is *la gloire* for yet another year.

Until quite recently women did not enter this contest - it would not even have occurred to them to do so in a male-dominated village society. Then, one or two of the more brave and liberated female souls tried to enter and were of course banned. But even in this remote spot the malign influence of the modern world cannot be denied access, and the *petanque* competitions are now grudgingly open to all. Even *étrangers* may enter. And so the rules are rigged to have preliminary rounds in the hope that this will lead to an early elimination of the running sore of women and *étrangers,* thus enabling our heroes to continue as before. More often than not this ploy works, but it has been known for either or both to continue into the final rounds, and, horror of horrors, some *étrangers* have had the temerity to win against the odds.

If they are male, this is gritted-teeth acceptable. But the idea that a female, worse a female *étrangère*, might win is anathema. The shock to the collective male village ego would engender such a deep sense of shame that it would ruin the whole festival weekend To my knowledge this has not yet happened, but it can now only be a matter of time before the last vestiges of village masculine dignity are torn to shreds by the new enlightened world order.

The afternoon competition done and the annual champions acclaimed once more, the Saturday evening festivities repeat the pattern of the previous evening's excesses - loud music, frantic dancing, copious food and free-flowing wine. Sunday morning is a time for reflection. The village awakens with the retribution of a mass headache and goes to church in search of spiritual solace, tranquillity and grace. The pews are full of serially throbbing heads and aching bodies, betrayed only by the half-closed eyes and the occasional grimace of distress. But they must attend because, even at this painful time, tradition obliges the priest to bless the whole festival and to dispense low-cost and high-profile communion and forgiveness to an unusually quiescent congregation.

But afterwards, the power of prayer once more demonstrates its capacity to surmount human weakness. Now sanctified and shriven, the men of the village organise a *grillade*, or perhaps even the traditional Catalan version of this, the *cargolade*. This repast entails the immolation of hundreds of *escargots* over a charcoal fire. A British-educated stomach might begin to get alarmed at this, especially after the experience of the previous two days. Buckets and buckets of unlucky arthropods are collected weeks before the festival. Leaves are overturned, walls are examined, for slow-moving objects within three kilometres of the village. There is no hiding place despite all their efforts to blend into the village scenery. Those that escape, and there must be some to act as the Adams and Eves of next year's party, are probably brainier than most of the villagers. Those that don't are subjected to a diet of thyme and milk to cleanse them of any waste or toxic matter.

For the snails this is time of peace and reflection when food and drink no longer has to be laboured for. But the reckoning is at hand. The unfortunate nemiatoads are then spread out on a metal net to prepare them to meet their doom. As the flames complete their culinary task, it is now time for the younger men of the village to demonstrate their uninhibited masculinity by eating them in bountiful quantities. The average Briton might think that one is too many - but for these young men, eager to prove their macho credentials to the opposite gender, 50, 100, 150 is normal. Some have been known to eat more than 250 snails at one sitting, thus demonstrating to all and sundry a) their staying power, b) their potency and c) their stupidity.

Females tremble at such feats of voracity, but they have little need to worry, since any aphrodisiac attribute the snails may have had is soon dissipated by the inevitable effects of over-indulgence. Full stomach never won fair lady – and certainly not one full of creatures that produce slime trails, 'twas ever thus. The young men fade miserably, often urgently, from the scene. For the wiser villagers the *cargolade* continues in more sedate fashion with pork chops and the spicy sausages called *merguez*, which, again if consumed in too large a quantity, can have much the same effect as the snails.

Before the last of the festival hops, there is a performance of the *Sardane*, the traditional dance of the Catalan regions. For this, the larger villages will hire a *cobla*, a group playing the traditional pipes and instruments of the region. The smaller ones will use scratchy records played on an ancient gramophone set – the type grandma used to have. The *Sardane* is not an easy dance for the uninitiated. It is performed in a circle in which people join hands, men's supporting the ladies. It starts with four basic simple steps, hands joined by the sides. After 84 beats (one must learn to count before dancing the *Sardane*) the arms are raised above head height and the dance proper commences with a complex series of steps repeated over and over again.

As it reaches its climax the music subtly changes to a more vibrant rhythm, and an animated high-stepping commences. This too is performed within a similarly complex pattern of steps but the trick is to give the impression of temporarily floating on air, everyone landing at the same time. . It isn't easy. It is an impressive sight when done well, though village festivals are not always the perfect stage for precision.

Men and women dance together unselfconsciously, justly proud of their terpsichorean heritage. It is a beautiful and timeless expression of a whole nation and one hopes that it will survive the predations of these cynical times. Even in this frenetic day and age the local towns and villages organise Sardanes in the evening so that workers can indulge their tradition on their way home. It is difficult to imagine that happening outside the Westminster underground station or the Greenock shipyard at knocking-off time.

Often, unsuspecting tourists are dragged into the fray, their clodhopping efforts to match the steps of their tutors contrasting strongly with the delicate and elegant steps of the cognoscenti. Each August, the town of Ceret over the hill organises a popular annual competition. The 28th festival of the Sardane this year attracted more than 100 teams from schools and villages all over the *Pyrenees-Orientales département,* and beyond from Spain.

However, back to the Conflent village festival. It ends, as it began with an ear-splitting rave-up. Those with energy remaining - the tennis players, the under-30s, the hyperthyroidic and the simply masochistic - party the night away, happy in the knowledge that not only are they having the best time since the last one, and before the next one, but also that the whole valley is reverberating with them in their pleasure.

The poetic version of this story goes like this, written in the style
of a Lancashire monologue

Village Celebrations - a Conflent Monologue.

Here in the Conflent we celebrate well
We do little else if the truth is to tell
So here's how we do it, a tale of romance
In this beautiful region of south-western France

May is the time when the French have a ball
And holiday most of the month, if not all
There's Mayday, VE day, Ascension and Whit
So they add a few extra to make a nice fit

But all through the summer there's an annual affair
To celebrate saint's day in each village square
If the Saint's day's in winter that's no immense sweat
There's another in summer when the weather's not wet

They start Friday evening when the band passes by
And piles up its blasters eleven feet high
The square is emblazoned in dazzling light
To remind all the people that this is their night

Round about ten the village bells clang
And the party begins with an almighty bang
The decibels thunder, the ear-splitting sound
Rings out through the village and valley around

The villagers rock and they roll and they hop
For 3 or 4 hours through the night without stop
In the eaves and the barns the mice and the rats
Rock and roll too with the dogs and the cats

The young and the fit, the middle aged too
Holiday visitors, Brits passing through
A gyrating, vibrating maelstrom of mass
Trapped in a humanoid dancing impasse

All save the wrinklies, the boppers of yore
Who can't even manage a waltz anymore
Deaf as a post and blood pressure high
It's at times like these that they understand why.

Buildings and pavements vibrate with the tunes
A few more large cracks will appear very soon
But who cares, this night is the hedonist's dream
Tomorrow will tell if it's been too extreme

The food tables heave next door to the bar
Enough fatty plaques to turn brains into tar
The only main drawback is no-one can hear
Whether they want a hot-dog or a beer

Saturday morning the village is still
The middle-aged rockers all feel rather ill
Their bones ramrod stiff and their heads in a spin
Pain racks their bodies and tempers are thin

The youngsters are staying in bed until two
Because that's what modern young people can do
Only the wrinklies are wandering the lanes
Last nights excesses have addled their brains

But the silence is short for, in line with tradition
The afternoon sees a petanque competition
When all macho men who like to act big
Will throw metal balls at a little white pig.

Alas times have changed even here in this land
Etrangers and women can now try their hand
Sex liberation's the name of the game
Much to the men's notion of ultimate shame

They'll lose to a stranger as long as he's male
But to lose to a woman is beyond the pale
So they organise contests to weed out the scourge
They do it in vain, for the pests still emerge

Up and down wander the contestant teams
Seeking to win the trophy of dreams
The winner is known, the arbiters summon
The men praise the lord. It isn't a woman!

At 9 pm sharp it's back to the square
For another long night of melodious fare
All is a frenzy of colour and light
A mingling, jingling and swingalong night.

The morning of Sunday sees mass retribution
Time to seek pardon and beg absolution
The church pews are filled with sore throbbing heads
And the pain almost makes them wish they were dead.

The priest gives the blessing, forgiveness is rife
Spiritual solace will offer new life
The people, now shriven, continue the search
For saints' weekend fun by the grace of the church.

The power of prayer works its wonders once more
A cargolade's planned and there's feasting in store
Buckets and buckets of unlucky snails
Have been gathered together in hundreds of pails

For these silent creatures there's no hiding place,
On walls, under leaves in every crawlspace
The villagers find them wherever they lurk
Wherever they play, wherever they work

Thyme and milk help prepare for the reckoning
It won't be long now, for snail heaven is beckoning
For them this is space for peaceful reflection
On the meaning of life and achieving perfection

The square is now covered with long trestle tables
The wiser ones sit where the ground is more stable
These are now garnished with bottles of wine
For thirsty consumers an inspiring sign

The men find the wood and kindle the fire
The arthropods spread on a griddle of wire
They barely have time to request supplication
Before they experience slow immolation

It's enough to turn the Brit stomach to dust
But snails in these parts are creators of lust
The young men all drivel in anticipation
Aphrodisiac snails raise a high expectation

Their manhood depends on how many they eat
Eighty, a hundred's a wonderful feat
Expectancy grows with each snail consumed
It's now that the promise of heaven's assumed

Females tremble at such great voracity
But too many snails promotes incapacity
The young men all exit in desperate grief
And the women all breathe a huge sigh of relief

The feast then continues with sausage and chop
Until the red wine causes eyelids to drop
A brief snooze is needed to refresh one within
It's time once again for the dance to begin

But before this there's time for the graceful sardane
The national dance of the true catalan
Performed in this region for centuries past
And one of the few old traditions to last

The villagers form a series of rings
Hands joined together like puppets on strings
As the music begins they all move as one
Intricate patterns are traced on the stone

The music continues, the rhythms advance
And a high-stepping movement takes over the dance
It isn't easy, like floating on air
And landing together with exquisite flair

The Brits and the visitors, Barbarian bands
Join in the party to try out their hands
Their clod-hopping efforts are pathetic to see
The poise of a dead cow and the grace of a flea

And so to the ball, masochistic delight
Those left with energy dance into the night
The hyperthyroidoic, the sportive, the brave
Push the heart's limits for just one last rave.

A willing and milling, thrilling commotion
Of swirling, whirling bodies in motion
Till even the fittest runs out of puff
And the band decides that enough is enough

And that is the typical Conflentais fête
One that the people will never forget
Time for one mouthful of red wine or beer
'Till the village is silent again for a year

©Norman Longworth

And that has been the Conflent way of celebrating over the centuries. While sound technology may have inflated the decibel count in modern times, there is still inherent in these festivals a symbolism which runs deep into the psyche of the people, and which holds the village together as a community. Inter-generational disputes are set aside for the duration. Sadly, in many parts of France, and indeed in Europe, these traditions and values are not resistant to the more urgent batterings of the media society, but here in le *Conflent profond* they remain for the time being

As an immigrant from the barbarian lands of the North, I sometimes believe that I have gone to sleep and woken up in Paradise, a lost valley somewhere between England and Spain, where ancient customs survive in a land of eternal sunshine and pleasure. It isn't all like that of course, as the other stories in these volumes will reveal, but I can tell you this. After twenty years in this valley I am, in my own heart, no longer an immigrant – I am an active, enthusiastic, paid-up *Conflentais*, as proud of the local catalan traditions as any born and bred local. I am captivated, passionate, addicted, absorbed, infatuated, engrossed, besotted, smitten by the people of this land and by the treasures I have found and have yet to find.

Of course as far as the locals are concerned, this is an impossible dream. They will wait at least another hundred years before passing judgment on my bona fide credentials to become an honorary catalan, and then another hundred to have them confirmed. And they will never understand why I am not living among my extended family in the ice-cold huts of terra Britannica. But the reality is that I am here, with my long-suffering wife, my bewildered dog and about seven hundred other would-be pseudo-catalans. The other immigrants will hate me for blowing the gaffe on their little secret, but in all truth I could not hold it back any longer. So that's my tale. It has a beginning and a continuation, but as yet no visible ending. And long may it remain so. The gory details will be filled in in subsequent tales. Happy Reading.

TALES OF THE CONFLENT

Chapter the Second

The Wyfe of Eus's Tale Part 1
or
Home Sweet Home

Being the story of how a Conflent dwelling-place became transformed into the very centre of the universe

The Wyfe of Eus's Tale – Life in Paradise

My husband, the self-styled ymmygrant, daft nutter, has described how we came to live in this paradise. I wondered when I would get a turn to tell my story. That guy rambles on and on like a gossiping housewife. Like I said, calls himself an Ymmygrant – there's posturing pretentiousness for you. But then he's a Pisces, forever in a dream of his own making, I'm a Taurus, one of those people who brook no bull-shit. So here's my chance to tell it my way, the practical, no-nonsense method. So no more nonsense - let me show you a little bit more about my house and how living in the Conflent transforms everyone of its immigrants, note no y's – my feet are firmly planted on the ground - into active hedonists.

For my sins, and my pleasure, I live in the commune of Eus, and here's why. I'll never forget that first view of the village from the Route nationale 116. It was enough to make a blind dog gasp, so unexpected was it. We left behind the village of Marquixanes and crossed the railway line up the valley onto the straight but undulating road towards the town of Prades (of which more later). A couple of hundred metres more and there it was on the right hand side. The vision, the village of Eus, a granite wedding cake fashioned by a semi-drunk chef who knew what he wanted to do but couldn't quite get the lines right. In clear weather, which is the norm for much of the time in the *Conflent*, its layers presented to my admittedly unsophisticated eye, a strange Escher-drawn three dimensional portrait situated, as it is, on a rocky outcrop of the near-distance hills, with its baroque church playing the part of the fairy on top.

Eus – one of the 'plus beaux villages de France'

It may not be the most gaspworthy village in France - after all, during our sojourn in Paris in the 1980s my husband and I had toured the hexagon from top to bottom, corner to corner, side to side, up and down. We have feasted our eyes upon the vertical splendour of Rocamadour, marvelled at the medieval magnificence of Riquewihr and stood in awe at the soaring volcanic majesty of Le Puy en Velay. But it is as well that it isn't any of these gems of architecture, since my first observation of what was to become my very own village was while driving the car. The driver's tale will put the reader au fait with the finer arts of catalan driving. It is not a pretty sight. The local driving manners and mores are well-known throughout France. Whereas most Brits regard French drivers as dangerous imbeciles who shouldn't be allowed behind a spinning wheel, the Catalans are the French driver's French driver. Catalan cars, irrespective of final destination, can appear at any point on the road at any time, their drivers seemingly unaware that only one car can occupy one slot in the space-time continuum at the same time. Quantum theory may question this assumption but this is the deep south, *la France profonde*, where quantum theory is more about the price of peaches. Add to this the summer multiplicity of tourists, each one gawping, like me, at the sudden vista of a *village perché* apparently glued precariously to the side of a steep hill and one has a recipe for potential disaster. I looked at the copious bunches of flowers seemingly placed at random at the side of the road and thought 'How pretty!' Little did I know at the time that these were the poignant evidence of yet another mortality statistic.

Searching for Paradise

But Eus is beautiful and so it came about that, on a warm balmy afternoon in October 1989, Helen, a strangely unassuming English estate agent, turned her car to the right off the Prades to Eus road into a small *chemin*. The journey continued for a short while along an avenue bordered by peach trees and with a view of the Canigou rising like a massive Disney Castle out of the plain. It turned a 90 degree bend, crossed a tiny country bridge over a tranquil stream, climbed a small rise, and said hello to a cherry orchard as it passed. This part of the journey took only one minute and covered only 300 metres.

Before us, on the left side of the little road, stood an unprepossessing faded ochre-painted mas, a farmhouse in the Catalan style. I glanced at my husband and saw the unmistakeable glint of discovery, such as might have appeared in the eye of David Livingstone on first contact with the Victoria Falls. St Paul himself could not have been more bowled over on the way to Damascus. He knew, I knew, we both knew that our future had been revealed to us. Even before the car pulled up, and even before the key in the door had been turned, we were both well and truly hooked.

Mas des Oliviers, as I later found its name to be, after the olive trees which once bedecked the countryside around, is situated in the commune of Eus and Comes. The latter is a deserted hamlet way up on the mountainside comprising 2 farmers, their sheep, several rabbits, a large number of bleating goats and some of the most vicious mosquitoes on God's earth. Eus is, by comparison a heaving metropolis of 368 souls give or take the odd monthly death and birth. There are many more of the former than the latter, the average age of its population topping the 70s with some ease.

My potential new habitation in this set-up wasn't exactly a divine revelation of enchanting and irresistible beauty either. Indeed it is plain and I suppose to some quite ugly. It had no crenellations, no ivy clambering up the walls, no flying buttresses, no baroque frontage - in fact no unusual features whatsoever, unless you count the pulley wheel over the top window. But within the limited budget we had set for our little piece of France, we could hardly expect the Palace of Versailles or the Chateau de Chambord.

 After having spent several days inspecting crumbling *maisons de village* entombed in narrow streets, where I could almost have washed in the bathroom of the house opposite, I was beginning to despair. In one place, we were pursued from house to house by hordes of wrinkly old ladies anxious to lower the mean age of the village by a few years. And we are by no means the most springlike of chickens. The previous house I had seen was roofless, no floorboards divided its three storeys and it sounded to me that we had interrupted the annual dinner of the woodworm association, so loud was the chomping and masticating.

I don't know what bon appétit is in woodworm-speak but they were certainly enjoying their lunch. Nevertheless it had a wonderful view of the sky and was a bargain at the price. In contrast, our new apparition of rural tranquillity was the stuff of visions and dreams. No doubt Helen, who had been an opera singer in a previous life, had exercised an expert estate agent's sense of theatre to captivate us in this way, but at the time the niceties of audience manipulation were not the first thing on our minds.

Let's be clear. Conflent farmhouses are predominantly functional. The ground floor is for animals, the middle floor for people and the upper floor for hay. Thus people become a sandwich between the warmth of their beasts and the warmth of the beast's food, though the arcane symbolism of this, if any, must be lost in the mists of time. This more recently re-constructed *mas,* re-built since the 1930s is more human-friendly, deploying the ground floor as a kitchen and garage, the animal economy of the old Conflent having been superceded by the growing of fruit.

The four rooms of the middle floor are for sleeping and the top floor is for entertaining visitors who can reach it. It has a slightly pitched roof and presents itself foursquare to the resplendent Canigou in the South, and fivesquare against our not-so friendly prevailing hurricane, the *tramontane*, which blows strongly and coldly, especially in winter, from the North-east. More about that later. This is not the only element the *mas* is built to withstand. The Eastern Pyrennees are reputed to be a region of geological instability, though I have felt the earth move, as an earthquake that is, only once in the time I have been here, and the next tremor isn't expected until well into the next decade. There lies a poignant metaphor for an aging couple.

But the major reason why the walls are stone-built and more than a metre thick is public enemy number one, the sun. While naive holiday-makers may come to these parts in search of a solar tan, the locals know only too well what it can do to a body. The houses are their only protection from its often relentless attack on this part of the earth's surface and these walls make the interiors wonderfully cool in summer and adequately warm in winter. The Catalans are forever ambivalent about the sun - it is both the source of what wealth they have and the curse of their labour. They both revere it and take every opportunity to escape from the object of their worship. When the sun does not shine they are the most miserable people on God's earth, and when it does they do their best to avoid it. It is one of life's small paradoxes in Eus which calls itself *le village le plus ensoleillé en France'*. And with an average of 310 sun days in a year who is there to gainsay that

Finding Nirvana

But, with houses, it is the interiors which reveal the person, and our initial encounter with the stomach *of le mas des oliviers* was no exception to the rule. When I first inserted a hesitant footstep through the entrance hall I wondered why I was suddenly blind. Everything was gloomy. I groped my way through a doorway into a black hole which I was told was the kitchen. I couldn't see a thing. Helen threw open the shutters and it was still dark, the radiant sun outside seemingly unable to make any sort of headway into the room. It was as if I had stepped into a mediaeval Hieronymous Bosch dreamscape.

At that point I realised how popular the sombre look is in France. As my eyes grew accustomed to the gloom, dark bisto-coloured wallpaper hung down, and sometimes off, each wall; the floor was covered in tiles that illustrated how the dark matter in every corner of the universe has its origins in the hidden recesses of the Catalan soul. The paintwork on doors and skirting board was even more Cimmerian than the wallpaper. A farmhouse chimney, complete with soot, along one wall seemed to radiate further darkness over an already dismal scene.

In the far corner, barely discernible in the gloom, stood a stone sink of the type usually seen in pictures of Victoriana surrounded by cherry-cheeked, heavy-bosomed washer-women - a sort of horsetrough with a draining-board in which one could scrub the week's washing, a fortnight's pots, the dog, the cat and the goat - all at the same time. Personally I thought it a very useful artefact in a household, but I detected the 'it goes or I do' gleam in my husband's eye - no washerwoman he! As my eyes grew accustomed to the lack of quality light, I glimpsed, in the corner on the right, a huge floor-to-ceiling cupboard. It was the sort of structure that Victorian children used to hide, or were hidden, in. My anxiety softened. After years of living in houses with insufficient storage space, here was a very heaven of a cupboard. I would have bought the house for that alone.

As I wandered, eyeless in Eus, into the dining room to be assailed by a similar panorama, I wondered if I should have brought special infra-red night glasses to view the house. It was as cheerful as a coal-hole at dusk on a rainy day. The pattern on the floor tiles could only have been designed by grinning demons in the nether reaches of Hades. A staircase of black and white marble temporarily alleviated the stygian image a little but, as I picked my way carefully up to reach the four bedrooms in the centre of the house, we were again plunged into the thick brown soup.

Each room made its own eloquent statement on the hopelessness of humankind's task to bring light and joy into the world. The bathroom was something else. Spacious it was not. Bath, shower, toilet and sink were engaged in a desperate struggle to find room to exist and not helped by the tiny slit in the wall which constituted a window. The previous occupiers, it seemed, had required privacy in their ablutions.

By contrast the enormous *grenier* on the top floor was a relative kaleidoscope of light, being devoid of both hay and wallpaper, except for two enormous rural wallcoverings dominating each alcove, the one of a sylvan glade deep in an unnamed forest and the other of a mountain scene such as is found on huge wall-sized chocolate boxes. This putative ballroom was empty of furniture save for a hospital bed of the 'torture-a-patient-for-Christmas' type, incongruously situated *en plein centre*. Salvador Dali could not have painted a more surreal scene.

A restoration tale

Such was my first view of the *mas* which is now the centre of my universe. So we bought it, much to Helen's, and my husband's, surprise. Now I may have been gender stereotyped as a girl but a lifetime of nursing has taught me that everything has its place and that there is a place for everything. So here was a challenge - to bring light into darkness, form into shapelessness and cheerful meaning into the opaque world of the Mas des Oliviers. The walls were solid, the structure sound and the roof in its rightful place.

Nothing a few tonnes of dulux and an active right arm couldn't cure. Outside was a vast expanse of shutters in similar decorative order, an overgrown garden and an impenetrable forest leading down to a stream, which Helen said she thought capable of holding trout. Three months later and several thousands of pounds poorer, we owned the property and the lost world surrounding it.

My first task was to mobilise some troops. And so the following Easter saw me drive with my husband from Cherbourg in one swoop and strike camp in one of the bedrooms with an open view of the *Canigou*. Two days later the first relief party, three cousins and an army of paintbrushes, rollers and wipers, arrived at Perpignan Airport. It is useful to have relatives in the paint business - in our case, confronted with a task of the tenth magnitude, it was absolutely essential. In our absence the local mason, on my orders, had made the wall between dining room and kitchen disappear in order to create a large farmhouse-style expanse covering three-quarters of the ground floor.

Filling it was a considerable challenge. In the initial two days, we had surveyed the second-hand shops and furniture stores of Perpignan (not an IKEA in sight) and requested delivery of the research findings a week forward. For the next ten days the passing farmers' tractors, which strangely seemed to quadruple the number of their journeys past the house, were privileged to observe a furious dance of frenetic artistic activity.

We dismantled, rubbed down, undercoated, top-coated twice and re-mantled several acres of shutter and casement window. We whitewashed, emulsioned and rolled gallons of white and pastel paint onto hectares of kitchen, staircase and bedroom wall. We stained and varnished two complete floors and transformed two-dimensional flat packs into three dimensional wardrobes, tables, beds and chairs, thus donating new life to each room.

We rose with the first lark and retired, whacked and weary, with the last nightingale. We ate, we drank and we worked, sustained by cordon bleu meals delivered by Roger, a Floyd manqué who, when in England, ran a fibre-glass company. My husband's favourite cousin, one of the most elegant ladies to be found in the whole of Merseyside, wallowed in paint, turpentine and grease like a contented hippopotamus in mud. She will not, by the way, enjoy that metaphor. We foolishly took a day off to renew ourselves in the Mediterranean waters at Collioure. On the way we bought £200 worth of food and 2 enormous tins of paint at the Auchan supermarket.

When we returned to the car all the food had disappeared, but the paint remained as a silent rebuke and as a reminder that we had transgressed two unwritten laws - thou shalt not leave food visible in a car at the seashore, it asketh to be taken, and thou shalt not enjoy thyself when thou shouldst be painting houses. When our angels of mercy upped brushes and departed after a superhuman effort, to a well-earned rest back in the workplace, Roger and Greg to the businesses they ran, Renee to the schoolroom she reigned over, the house had been totally re-fashioned into a gleaming pastel elysium, a dazzling testament to the power of paint, friendship and the right arm.

Two days later the phase two reinforcements arrived. Two friends from the golden metropolis of Wigan arrived, quickly followed by two students who had been attached to my husband for work experience in Belgium the previous year. The latter arrived after a night of standing upright on a crowded train, and so we gave them a restorative breakfast and immediately set them to work lugging heavy stones from the river to the house. It takes a certain amount of exquisite cruelty to be kind. The plan was to build a patio, an expanse of stone and concrete whereon we could al fresco the days and nights away. This was honest manly toil, blistered hands and lakes of perspiration.

Dave, an ex-headteacher, became mason for a week, laying and levelling, mixing and milling. Glen and Mick received a new form of work experience to round off their education, relinquishing the pen for the trowel and the computer for the wheelbarrow. For three days the west side of the house rocked with the hustle and bustle of a Wimpey construction project. Minutes after the patio was finished and the concrete had barely dried, we held a little opening ceremony complete with coloured string and scissors, while the local farmers looked on from the distance with glazed wide-open eyes. They had heard tales of the madness of *les anglais* and here was the proof before them. It was further confirmed as the site workers posed with arms folded, stomachs in and heads high for the victory photograph.

Job done! Grand Opening of the New Patio – Mason, labourers and supporters attending

The following day Glen and Mick deflowered the virgin slope and constructed a stairway to the nether world of the now-known-to-be-troutless stream. Meanwhile the work of unburdening the interior of the Mas of its Hadean darkness continued unabated and, by the time all hands had returned to the paint-free safety of England, the transformation was at least half-complete.

Tales of the metamorphosed Brits

Although, as I said, Catalan *mas* are neither the most beautiful nor innovative of architectural styles, they *do* have the most colourful roofs. A sort of baked earth red, they cascade from pitch to eave one tile underneath the other. They are the very devil to maintain, cracking or moving in the *tramontane* blow with a regularity which makes roofing a highly lucrative, and dangerous, business in the region. More than once, I have required my husband, who is unfortunately one of the more dimensionally challenged of human beings, to squeeze like a stream of toothpaste through the skylight window, bucket of sloppy mortar in hand, to re-stick a recalcitrant red tile displaced by the wind.

The height of the mas being about sixty feet above the extremely hard ground, he waits until the wind has ceased before performing this task. Moving earthwards at thirty-two feet per second per second is not high on his list of fun activities. On the journey to the offending object he inevitably disturbed or cracks another four or five of them, for which he needs mortarial reinforcements. When he finally poured himself back through the skylight into the safety of the house, another two or three tiles have let it be known that they will soon be the focus of another precarious voyage to its upper regions.

If all this physical activity seems to be out of character for such cerebral types, I am not alone in this. The most salient feature of Britons newly installed abroad is their ability to metamorphose themselves into beings they had never been before. I have been amazed at the transformation wrought among our friends in the Conflent.

A bank manager, who has for years dashed several miles from the opportunity to build a small garden wall in England becomes an expert bricklayer and stonemason overnight, constructing aqueducts and garages as if he were born to it. A training college lecturer, who had great difficulty in even recognising wood in Wales, has developed chisels and saws as extensions to his hands and fashions beautiful artefacts from the trunks of trees. A computer nerd has forsaken the keyboard for the spirit level and the adze. A new vocabulary passes their lips. The conversation is of stresses and soakaways, concrete and cutaways, rulers and runaways.

The nature of Christmas presents changes. Santa Claus receives desperate Conflent requests in English for concrete mixers, do-it-yourself plumbing kits, be-a-great-stonemason building instructions and step-by-step install your own swimming pool exercise books. The new virility symbol is the *tronçonneuse,* or chain-saw. When 2 or 3 Brits are gathered together with the prospect of wood in the offing it is like a scene from Clockwork Orange.

Each stands proudly wielding his chainsaw like the most macho forester. Educational philosophy and economic theory now pass them by - all of that nonsense was in a previous life and all that now matters is the next construction programme, the price of gravel and how many bricks can be laid on a pin-head in an hour. It is a tribute to the Lifelong Learning culture and an accolade to the chameleon-like adaptability of the human species to melt easily into new environments.

In the first 3 years my husband and I (note the royal inference) spent all our holidays adding value and beauty to the *mas*. The four bedrooms are named after the seasons and decorated accordingly, reds and bright cherries for the summer room; browns, yellows and golds for autumn; greens and pale peach-blossom for spring; blues and whites for the winter room. This inspiration comes mainly from me – my husband's sense of colour co-ordination is even worse than that of a dead mole, though he says that I simply don't appreciate the subtlety with which he introduce new colour concepts into the hum-drum scheme of things.

Pillar-box red is his favourite colour so that tells you something. He can conceive a hundred opportunities to use it to enhance the appearance of a door, a chimney or a patio floor. He says that it's a pity that such immense creativity is so easily dismissed, and compares himself to Salvador Dali, Picasso and Matisse, who he says were also once laughed at in the same way. What a piss-artist!

The balcony's tale

My *pièce de résistance* lies in the *grenier,* which has been converted into a giant salon-cum-patio. It is here that we have made our greatest constructional change to the *mas* by appending a balcony along its entire west wall. One approaches this from an internal loggia in the shape of a tetrahedron surrounded entirely by glass. Thus we can eat outdoors on the balcony and, if it is raining or too windy, close the sliding doors and eat with the outside still in view.

The effect of the irregular square is quite dramatic, giving an all-round reflection of the surrounding hills in the style of a diorama. It would be nice to say that this was entirely a design plan, but a lifetime of truth-telling forces me to reveal that the effect is as much accidental as it is deliberate. But it is a remarkable improvement. No matter that it was unplanned. No matter that our neighbour has complained twenty times to the Mayor that we now overlook his meadow (though, since it contains nothing but grass, it is difficult to know why this is an important drawback for him).

The salon, formerly a hayloft, looking towards the new loggia

The view now looks southward over the pear, peach and nectarine trees onto the mighty changing panorama of the Canigou; westwards, we preside over our garden and copse, observe from a distance the town of Prades two kilometres away and look out along the valley until, as far as the eye can see, we can glimpse the 17th century Fort Liberia above Villefranche; northwards we survey the rolling hills of the *Fenouillèdes*, fold after fold of mountain ridge rising to the village of Comes at 3000 feet and upwards beyond there. Eastwards we look on the one hand to our *village perché* of Eus and on the other to the village of Marquixanes, gateway to the Conflent. By night the views are equally seductive. The church of St Pierre in Prades gleams like a beckoning beacon, and Eus is a brilliant Christmas Tree of twinkling lights, an enchanted fairyland more splendid than anything Disney dreamed of.

We frequently entertain friends on the balcony. I'm a dab hand with the pots and pans and no mean cook either. As we tuck into the hors d'oeuvres the delicate evening luminescence is reflected in the polished lens of the loggia. During the main course, choirs of nightingales in the copse are competing madly for attention against the flow of human conversation. The cheese course is regally presided over by a Canigou of shifting blues and greys and blacks as the dusk takes hold of the surrounding earth. All the while the pudding - ah those puddings, usually a choice of at least three mouth-watering dishes - is accompanied by the rosy glow of the declining sun, bathing us in an ethereal lustre.

Or is it the wine? Whatever, it doesn't matter. Nothing matters at this juncture. As we all recline gracefully, the better to appreciate our *digestifs,* we have temporarily disembarked from the cruel world and extinguished the tyranny of transient time. Complacent and fulfilled we may be, but we'll wake up again tomorrow. And someone has to do the washing up, and we all know who that is! So I set my husband to work and contemplate the evening stars once more.

Our omni-purpose balcony has already experienced a rich history. Since there is no industry of any kind within many miles the air in the Conflent tends to be clear and clean. Each fold of the hills stands out in stark contradistinction, such that the impression of distance becomes foreshortened. Two strides would seem to be sufficient to cross the adjoining meadow, four more and we could be on top of the Canigou. This effect is especially marked in the cool, crisp winter evenings The Milky Way treads its irregular path across the velvet sky like a celestial right of way, a myriad stars of every magnitude almost hide the vacant expanses of the universe and their glow radiates swiftly over the aeons to provide light for our little chemin.

The Tale of the Etoiles Filantes (shooting stars)

There was the time of the *étoiles filantes,* shooting stars, last year. Billed in the local newspaper as a scene not be missed, the majority, it said, would be in the constellation of Ursa Minor at around 1 am. Now neither my husband nor I are Captain Kirk or Spock. We know how to find the North Star so that we can find our way back to England at night. We recognise the evening star, Arcturus, and the great heavenly triangle of Deneb, Altair and Vega. Beyond that we are guessing. Give us the captaincy of starship enterprise and we would be lost in a stardate second. So it was on the night of the *étoiles filantes*. As the clock struck one, we both arranged our sunbeds flat on the balcony, Artur between. My husband, as always, awaited events while I tried to order them better.

Armed with an extremely heavy Times Atlas of the world and a torch, I lay on my back and opened it at the star page, Northern Hemisphere. *'There it goes'* cried my husband as I tried to orient the book to fit the sky. I looked up. It had gone. *'Another'* he shouted as I lined up the Milky way in the book with the real one in the sky. *'Three at once there'*, he screamed excitedly, as I searched for Ursa Minor in the book, the better to identify whether I had it the right way up or not. Nothing seemed to fit - Arcturus had, strangely for a first magnitude star, disappeared to another quadrant, the north star had migrated to somewhere south-east of Canigou and ursa minor was, according to the book, somewhere in the middle of the Milky way in October.

This was September so at least the young animal should have been getting near it. As time proceeded, the book became heavier, the torch less accurate and my ability to identify the sky, let alone the stars, disappeared completely. After half an hour I gave up, and tried the husband method. But the show was over. All in all he reckoned to have seen about 25 shooting stars and even Artur had seen 5. Me, I had learned the names of a lot of new constellations and developed new atlas-holding muscles. Not one shooting star had I seen. That's what balconies are for.

July 14th – party time

I said too that we look over the church of Prades, some distance away. It is here that the local Catalans celebrate the fact that they are also French with a huge fireworks display every July 14th. One of the main differences between the two sides of Catalonia is the question of who they are. In Catalonia du Sud, which stretches from the Spanish border right down through Barcelona to the delta of the Ebro, people regard themselves as Catalan first and Spanish second - that is those who will even recognise that there is a second. Here in the Conflent they are without equivocation French first and Catalan second. The Catalan national day is the same as the English - 23rd April - and their patron saint is the same, St Jordi, dragon and all, though it is only celebrated strongly south of the border.

Anyway, to resume the story, July 14th is bastille day for the French and firework day for us britanniques who want to join in. This year we celebrated in style. We endured yet another Epicurean battering on the balcony, made by our Welsh cooking wizard. A round score of us feasted on some of the most scrumptious Chinese dishes it is possible for any human being outside, and probably inside, China to make. Then we who are members of the celebrated Eus chorale puffed and perambulated (we could proceed no faster) up the narrow cobbled streets of the village, with our groupies, to the Place de la Republique in order to brighten up everyone's day by singing a few lyrics. The weather was hot, very hot, but that served only to stimulate further the already well-established levels of alcohol consumption by all and sundry.

There, beneath the plane trees, surrounded by flower-bedecked cottages we sang. Canigou looked out over the valley, cocked a lazy ear and was pleased.

Canigou listens to our song

The late afternoon passed into early evening and, as everyone danced al fresco to the hot, cold and mixed rhythms of the Band'Eus, France and England settled forever their differences, Wales and Catalonia discovered a common Celtic heritage, Holland mediated and bought beverages for everyone in an orgy of European-ness. The hundred years war, the Napoleonic hegemony, the burning of Jeanne d'Arc by Burgundy, France and England, the burgers of Calais, the war of Jenkin's ear, seemed to have happened an uncountable long time ago and to have been a wicked waste of good drinking time.

As early passed into later evening, those who could still stand, and some who could not, came at 11 pm to watch the 10.30 firework display from the famous balcony. The oohs and ahs as rockets soared, exploded in the air and dispensed their sparkling messages of wonder neatly expressed our foreign appreciation to our French hosts for sharing their pride and their day with us. When we mention this to our French friends they reply - 'Mais monsieur, we are all Europeans now - we should all celebrate all our national days together!'. And what a good idea that is, even though a terrible retribution struck many of us quite forcibly on July 15th.

Fauna of the Conflent

Five of us share this Shangri-la in the Conflent. My husband is not quite so animal mad as me. He often wonders out loud – too loud – what a retired couple is doing sponsoring a whole vet at the local clinic. And I have to admit that the annual fees for keeping our animals in tiptop condition seem to be related to a branch of astronomy in financial terms. Artur will speak for himself in Volume 2, but we should also mention that four other animals act as time-wasters in this menage.

My husband and I have a system for acquiring pets. *I* propose a new one, my husband protests vigorously and applies the family veto on it. I appeal to his better nature and he denies having one. He refuses even to entertain the idea. The next day the newcomer arrives. Simple system, simple solution. He was not a dog lover until Artur put paid to that. But, as for pets of the feline variety, he has barely a good thing to say about them. In his embittered view, they all get in the way of the good things in life like travelling and relaxing.

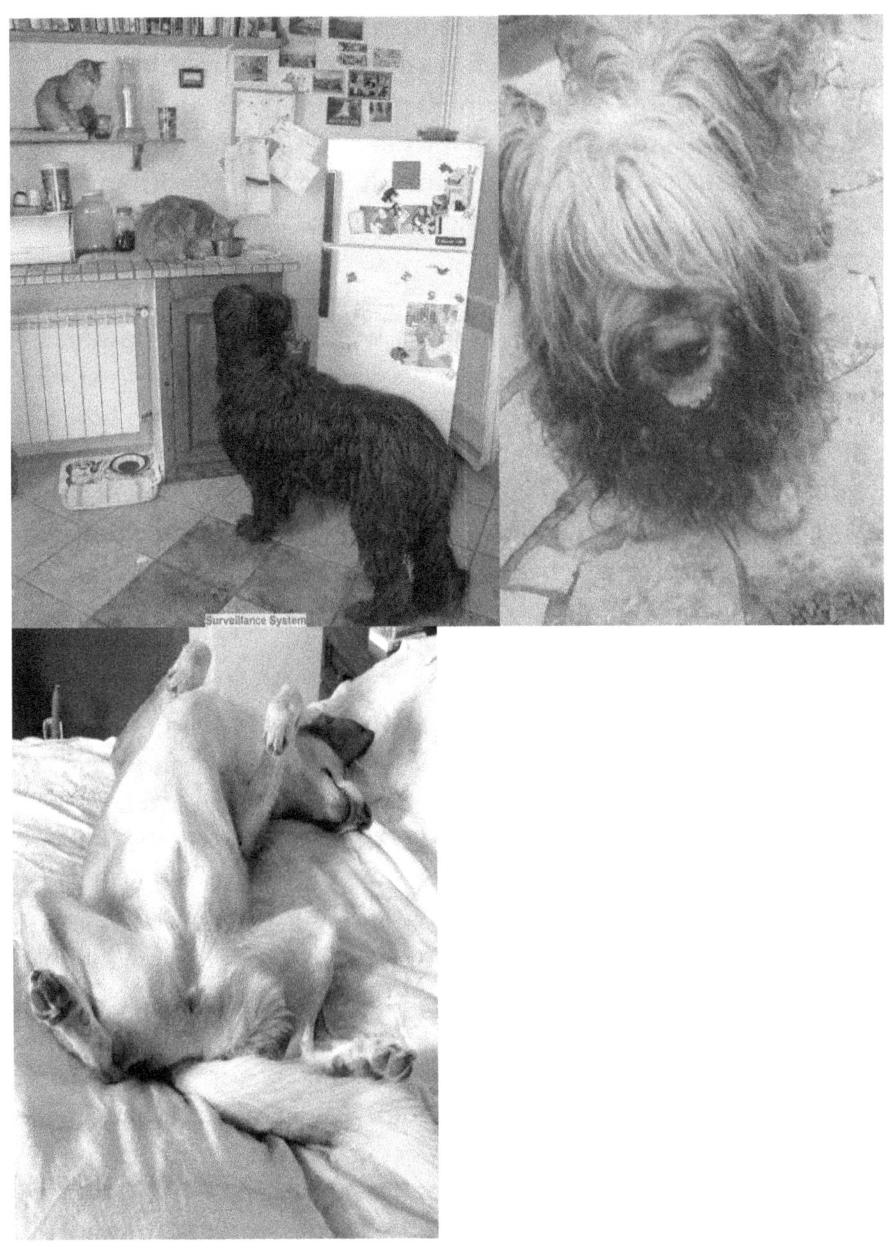

Let me at'em - feeding time at the zoo. Former inhabitants of the mas des oliviers menagerie

Artur is different. He even gets to choose the car we have. 'But will Artur like it?' is the question forever on our lips each time we replace the clapped-out vehicle which previous dogs have ripped to pieces. So we bring Artur along for the test ride and if he doesn't bite the salesman, we don't take it. Not true of course, Artur only bites sheep, it's in his nature. It's just that some people look, and behave, like sheep.

He is especially fond of the young ewes who sway their brightly dressed trousers from side to side. He's as good at pinching such bottoms as any Italian gigolo. The innocent look he puts on his face afterwards has to be seen to be believed. The ewes are not always best pleased by such attentions. Some of them look accusingly at my husband as if he had done it, but he too has the knack of innocence, or maybe he just looks too knackered even to contemplate such an action, and they wander on shaking their heads at the mystery.

The other two animals are cats and the only way I can influence their presence is by getting him to name them. This is the agreement we have. I gets the pets, he calls them names. The black cat, my *bête noire* so to speak, is Grimethorpe, so named not because of his colour, but more because my husband was listening to the colliery band of that name on a CD when he arrived. We wager there aren't many other cats of that name, even in Yorkshire.

We first came into contact with him in a field chez some friends of ours in Los Masos. They had been feeding him while in their mountain refuge for four weeks and were looking around for some soft touch to take over. His siblings had been eaten by a fox and this tibbles was the only survivor. I of course arrived at the crucial moment in this story. It wasn't just the eleventh hour. It was three seconds to twelve and they were packed ready to leave. So tibbles became Grimethorpe and the rest is history. The friend actually attended the same school as my husband so there was a touch of the old boys' code about it.

Grimethorpe has another distinction and that is that his name is completely unpronounceable by our French neighbours and friends. Once, when the cat strayed down to the mill by the Têt, I received a telephone call from a person unknown asking if I was Madame Greemtorp. At first the penny refused to budge, until she realised that some kind soul had found the cat and confused the name on his disk with the name of his owner. As I said, he's a survivor. And you can read his story in Volume 2 Chapter 8.

The other cat arrived unheralded and unwelcomed. For two nights we had been kept awake by a plaintive bleating which never seemed to stop. It sounded as if a herd of lambs had invaded our garage. The third night we investigated and found a small grey and white kitten under the freezer in the corner. I fed him and asked around all the people in the neighbourhood. But everyone responded as if I was asking them how they would like to help care for patients in the great plague. The second day it made a huge leap from the balcony and hared off into fields as if it were attached to a homing beacon. So I thought no more about it. One week later he was back, still bleating and thinner than ever. I believe that he had been abandoned by someone going away on holiday.

Well, what can one do? I again sent out a search party for my husband's better feelings and so Tarzan signed on the dotted line for the family menagerie. He first wanted to call him Greystoke on account of his colour, but that sounds too much like Grimethorpe, so he is now Greystoke's alter ego, Tarzan, and has proved that he can live up to it by his prodigious leap. The balcony is now surrounded by small-mesh fencing to preclude a repeat performance. He is still highly traumatised by his experiences in his short life to date and will disappear under the chair every time someone blows his nose, but I am a very good dispenser of t.l.c.

and he'll also survive. The sight of me at the front door trying to attract the cats - here calling Grimethorpe and there Tarzan is one of the Conflent's unsung wonders. And I'm still awaiting the phone call which says 'Is that Madame Tarzan?' I have my answer all ready and prepared.

Now that I'm in full flow, there's obviously so much more to tell. My husband diagnoses a bout of verbal diarrhoea but what the hell does he know, and when did I ever take notice of him? So maybe you can get to read part 2 of my paradise memoirs in the volume 2 if you thought that this first one was too good to be true. It gets even better there.

TALES OF THE CONFLENT

Chapter the Thyrd

The Honda's Tale

A play in 3 Acts

Being the story of the adventures of a 1989 Honda Civic in the war of the French bureaucracy

The Conflent Tales

Chapter 3 – The Car's Tale (as told by its owners, since most cars are unable to speak or write)

In case we give the impression that living in the Conflent is all pleasure, privilege and self-gratification we insert a cautionary tale. The French bureaucracy has a world-wide reputation for - well, bureaucracy, and we can verify that it is all true. Consider the simple story of naturalising the left-hand drive Honda Civic car which we brought over to France, after having previously taken it from Belgium to England.

The Japanese Car and the Carte Grise- a playlet in three acts.

Act 1 Scene 1 - The dwelling of an Insurance Agent in Prades

We: Good morrow, kind sir, we would perforce insure our vehicular transport, which recently from England is come.

Agent: (rubbing hands) 'Tis well good people that thou hast found my humble abode. May God strike me dead if I cannot give thee a good deal. Pray, what is the marque of this vehicle.

We: Why, 'tis a Honda, of the type they call Civic.

Agent: (a little more severe) A Japanese car, I'll warrant. 'tis a pity 'tis not French. Still, let us consult the oracle which dispenses wisdom to all things (turns to computer screen - all bend forward) Let us pray - Oh mighty Computer, we beseech thee to give us this day an answer to the question which we so urgently crave. Make it one which is acceptable to them and to me, especially the latter. Amen. Now let us enter the information which will assuredly cause this blessed machine to answer our prayers.

We: In truth, here are the documents you require to feed the blessed machine.

(Pause while agent taps information into Computer)

Agent: Now let us offer unto it a summary of your wishes. Fully comprehensive?

We: Oui!

Agent: Recovery?

We: *Bien sûr!*

Agent: Any driver?

We: Non, we are but two.

Agent: Bien, let us now prepare to receive the results of the mighty oracle's wisdom. (presses return button with flourish and sits back. Others bend forward further). Voilà. 1500 euros, not bad huh?

We: (Gulping) Assuredly it is more than double than in our last country, but we have sampled the driving in this region and can understand why there should exist such a large yearly premium.

Agent: Yearly? Ah, you jest - the famous British sense of humour is it not? This is of course for 6 months.

We: (Brows furrowed and moist) Perhaps, kind sir, you have omitted to account for the no claims bonus. We are both safe drivers and in England we had the benefit of a 60% no claims bonus.

Agent: Ah. Assuredly it does not contain provision for the bonus, but this would be a matter for the underwriter to determine and you would have to furnish the proof.

We: (searching in handbag). Indeed we were prepared for such eventualities and have brought the testimony from our insurance companies for the past 7 years.

Agent: Verily, you are well prepared, (looks at documents) But these are in English.

We: Indeed so. That would be because they were provided in England, but examine also the Belgian document. That too is written in English. The two amount to a testimony of 7 years of impeccable driving without accident and, if it so helps, perforce we may provide evidence of a further 30 years, if we can but recall the insurance companies we have used.

Agent: Seven years? Why for that I can give you a bonus of 30%. But let me complete one more item of information. What is the registration number of your car?

We: Why, it is C765RRU. But in England we had a bonus of.....

Agent: That is forsooth a strange number and not French. I regret that I will have to add 100 euros to the premium.

We: But please say why. Though the numbers on the *plaque d'immatriculation* may differ, yet we will not drive the car in any but our most careful way.

Agent: I regret that this rule of the company irks you. However, the matter is easily settled. You can obtain a French *Carte Grise* for the car and this will give you a French number plate. I will not charge this extra premium if you complete that in the first month.

We: Indeed this is a wondrous solution. How could such an end be obtained?

Agent: I regret I know not the way to do it, but, *en principe*, the Post Office might assist your search. Shall I issue a provisional certificate?

We: (tired and dispirited) We suppose so. Thank-you for your time and kind advice. (exeunt all)

Scene 2 - the Post Office in Prades ten minutes later

We: Verily this is a long queue.

Customer: Yes it is the custom and the system. Every letter to be despatched must go through the computer before franking, thus increasing fourfold the passing time.

We: (twenty minutes later) At last we have arrived at the counter. We would, kind Sir, like to buy a *Carte Grise* for our car recently imported from England. These are the documents.

Counter Clerk: In truth, monsieur, we cannot do that here. You should hie you to the Sous-Prefecture. It finds itself on the Route Nationale not far from here.

We: Thank-you for your time and kind advice (exit door left)

Scene 3 - outside the Sous-Prefecture 10 minutes later

Me: The place would seem to be closed. Let us read this notice here on the wall. It says 'Open to customers on Tuesday morning and Thursday afternoon.' Why, today is Friday. Verily we shall have to wait until next Tuesday to obtain our Carte Grise. (exit)

Scene 4 - The entrance hall of the Sous-Prefecture. 9 am Tuesday morning.

Me: 'Twould seem to be deserted and quite devoid of information as to the proper place for obtaining a new *Carte Grise.*

Maggie: Lo, here comes a young lady let us ask her where we should go. Excuse me, madame, can you please tell us where the room for obtaining a *Carte Grise* may be found?

Young Lady: Ah you are English are you not. I know not the answer to your question but this I do know. Before you can obtain a *Carte Grise* you will need proof of residence in France. This can be obtained from your Mairie.

We: But we live in Eus

Young Lady: Then it is to the Mairie of Eus that you must go.

We: Thank you, Madame, for your time and kind advice.

Scene 5 - Outside the Mairie at Eus - thirty minutes later

Me: It would seem that it is closed, but first let me read this notice outside. It says 'Open every afternoon except Tuesday.' It would seem that we will have to wait until tomorrow afternoon to obtain the wherewithal for our *Carte Grise*.

Scene 6 - Inside the Mairie at Eus - Wednesday afternoon

Mayor's Secretary: Have you an appointment?

Me: No, I regret that I did not know that we needed one. Please accept our apologies.

Mayor's Secretary: No matter, no-one is here for the moment. How can I help you?

We: We have come to confirm our residence in France so that we may procure a *Carte Grise* for our imported car.

Mayor's Secretary: Ah yes. For that you will have to make application for a *Carte de Séjour*, which confirms you as resident in our commune. These are the necessary papers. When you have completed them return them to me and I will send them further to the prefecture in Perpignan. In their turn they will send you a *récépissé* which will be confirmation that you have applied.

We: How long will this thing take?

Mayor's Secretary: I cannot say, but this I do say. I will send them immediately you give them to me.

We: Thank-you, madame for your time and kind advice. (exit door right)

Scene 7: Chez nous:

Me: (on telephone) Hello, is that the Insurance Agent? We have encountered some problem with the *Carte Grise*. We have to wait the processing of our application for a *Carte de Séjour.* This may take time.

Insurance Agent: (voice on telephone - cheerily) It matters not. We can wait. *Bonne chance.*

Act 2 Scene 1 - chez nous. Friday.Two weeks later.

Maggie: The postman has just delivered our daily mail and lo, here is a letter from the Prefecture in Perpignan. (opening the letter) Why 'tis the *récépissé* we have been awaiting.

Me: At last, we can now go to the *Sous-Prefecture* for our *Carte Grise* and afterwards pass by the Insurance Agent.

Scene 2 - Tuesday Morning. Inside the *Sous-Prefecture.*

Me : I wonder what the system is for obtaining *Cartes Grises.* I'll just knock on this door and ask.

Madame (a little crossly at being disturbed): Oui monsieur?

Me: We have finally obtained our *récépissé* and have come with our car documents to acquire a *Carte Grise* for our imported car. (shows documents)

Madame: (sniffily) I'm sorry monsieur. You are mistaken. I cannot help. *Cartes Grises* are dealt with at the office of the *Préfecture* in Perpignan.

Me: But that is a journey of more than 45 kilometres.

Madame: (lips pursed) I'm sorry monsieur. That is the system. Here is the address.

Me: Thank you for your time and kind advice.

Scene 3   At the *Préfecture* in Perpignan one hour later

Maggie: God, this is a dark and dismal place. And why does it seem that the whole of Perpignan is here?

Me: They have much to do in the *Préfecture*. Let us ask this lady if she can tell us where to obtain our *Carte Grise*? Pardon, Madame we have come from Prades to obtain a *Carte Grise* for our imported car.

Lady at desk: I see. What sort of a car is it?

Me: It is known as a Honda Civic.

Lady at desk: Oh dear. It is a Japanese car. Does it have a *Certificat de Conformité*?.

Me: I expect so, madame, we have retained all the documents from when the car was first purchased. But what exactly is that?

Lady at desk: It is a certificate that the car is licensed to be driven on French Roads

Me: Well, it is a left-hand drive car and it has been driven with no impediment on Belgian and English roads. And, more, when we lived in Belgium, we drove it for thousands of kilometres on French roads.

Lady at Desk. I'm afraid that you don't understand monsieur. It has to have a specific certificate applicable to the car. However, it is not my place to tell you this. Here is a number. Wait until it is displayed on the screen and then enter yonder office.

Me: Thank-you for your time and kind advice. Shall we wait for a seat?

Lady at desk: If one becomes free you are welcome to sit on it, but I wish you *bonne chance*.

Scene 4   The *Préfecture* in Perpignan two hours later.

Man at desk: Are you number 96?

Me: Oui monsieur.We have been waiting two hours.

Man at desk: (aside) Only that. What can I do for you?

Me: We have come to purchase a *Carte Grise* for our imported car, so that we may change the number on the plates and not be subject to additional premium on our insurance. We have the *récépissé* which gives proof that we have applied for a *Carte de Séjour,* and all the Car documents.

Man at desk: OK. Let me examine what you have. (looks through documents). Oh dear. It seems that you lack some essential papers. Have you paid the TVA?

Me: Yes, of course monsieur. There in front of you is the TVA certificate we obtained when we acquired it in Belgium.

Man at desk: I regret that that is not sufficient. You will need a French certificate that there is no more TVA to be paid. You will have to contact your local tax office in Prades. Has the car been submitted for a *Contrôle Technique*?

Me: Oui monsieur. We had one such completed in the week before we left England. There is the certificate. I understand the English ones to be more rigorous than the French.

Man at desk: (sucking air through teeth) I'm afraid that will not do monsieur. The certificate is in English and the car will have to undergo a French *Contrôle Technique*. I don't see a *Certificat de Conformité* here. It is a Japanese car is it not?

Me: It is, and it has conformed to regulations in Belgium and England and has been driven many miles in France.

Man at desk: Again not enough monsieur. All Japanese cars must have a French *certificat de conformité* The local Honda dealer will be happy to assist.

Me: (With Sarcasm) Is that all. Do we not need individual certificates for the seats, the lights, the carburettor and the petrol cap?

Man at desk: That will all be sorted out at the *Contrôle Technique* Monsieur. Good-bye. Next.

We: Thank you monsieur for your time and kind advice.

Act 3 Scene 1 - At the Honda Dealer in Perpignan the following day.

Maggie: We have come to obtain a *certificat de conformité* for a Honda Civic.

Dealer (with interest): What sort of Honda Civic would you like to buy?

Maggie: You misunderstand. We already have the car. We imported it last month from England.

Dealer: (no longer interested) Imported? I'm sorry, Madame, I cannot give you a certificate for an imported car. That has to be despatched from Honda Headquarters in Paris. But I will give you the address so that you can write to them.

Maggie: Thank you monsieur for your time and kind advice.

Scene 2 - At the *Contrôle Technique* in Perpignan 30 minutes later.

Maggie: The *Préfecture* in Perpignan wishes this car to be submitted for a *Contrôle Technique*

Girl in Office: Oui, Madame, did you make an appointment?

Maggie: Oh dear no, Madame, should I have done?

Girl in Office: Oh oui Madame, we are very busy. But the mechanics will return at 3 pm after lunch. Perhaps you could come back then.

Maggie: I will. Thank you for your time and kind advice.

Scene 3 - At the *Contrôle Technique* one hour later.

Maggie: There seems to be an absence of cars at present. Perhaps it would be possible to fit me in.

Girl in Office: Ah oui, Madame, we have had some cancellations this afternoon. Please drive the car round there and I will record the details.

(Maggie drives car to inspection area and leaves it - half an hour passes)

It is complete now. There was only one minor fault and that should be put right within 3 weeks. Here is the certificate. That will be 80 euros.

Maggie: Thank you, madame, for your time and kind advice and the certificate.

Scene 4 At the Hotel des Impôts in Prades three days later

Me: We have come at the advice of the prefecture to obtain a certificate of VAT clearance for our imported car.

Official: (suspiciously) Imported eh? I see it is a Japanese car bought in Belgium and yet has been imported through England.

Me: Yes. we lived in Belgium and then went home to England. Now we intend to live in la belle France.

Official: (obviously impressed by the last phrase) . I see. And did you pay VAT in Belgium? -

Me: Oui, monsieur, here is the VAT certificate.

Official: Ah yes, VAT was higher in Belgium than France at the time. And did they ask for VAT in England?

Me: Non.monsieur

Official: And how old is the car?

Me: Seven years, monsieur

Official: C'est bon. No VAT to pay. Here is your Certificate. By the way, have you had the security numbers printed on it?

Me: Huh?

Official: The security numbers. It's necessary for all new cars and all imported cars to have the chassis number etched onto the windscreen and the side window.

Me: But no-one said anything at the *Contrôle Technique.*

Official. They wouldn't have noticed. I advise you to get it done as quickly as possible.

Me: Thank-you for your time and kind advice.

Scene 5   Chez nous two weeks later

Me: It is good that the man at the tax Office told us about the security numbers. It may have cost us another 100 euros but at least we will not be turned away at the prefecture again.

Maggie: Right, and there's a letter in the post at last from Honda in Paris. That will be our last document. It's in French what does it say?

Me: (between gritted teeth) It says 'Dear Sir, thank you for your letter requesting a *certificat de conformité*. Please send the following documents together with a payment of 150 euros. Yours etc.

We (exasperated): Oh no. Another two weeks delay. We'll have to tell the Insurance Agent.

Me (on telephone): Hello, is that the the insurance agent. Listen we have another delay.. Two more weeks will be needed to get the *Carte Grise.*

Voice of Insurance Agent (cheerfully): That's OK monsieur, we'll extend the deadline. *Bonne chance*!

Scene 7 The Prefecture in Perpignan two weeks later.

Man at desk: Are you number 165?

We: We are and finally we have all the documents to obtain our *Carte Grise*.

Man at desk: Let me see, Yes, That's OK , yes the TVA certificate, yes I see you have the *certificat de comformité*. Have you been to the Service des Mines?

Me: Hello again What is that?.

Man at desk: It's the public organisation in Rivesaltes where you have to go to check that your car conforms to the the *certificat de conformité* you have received. I'm sorry but I cannot give you a *Carte Grise* without that confirmation.

Me: So you now want a certificate to certify that the certificate of conformity conforms to the car's certificate of conformity. Isn't that just a teensy bit pushing bureaucracy to the limits of madness?

Man at desk: I'm sorry monsieur

Me: *You're* sorry! It's us that have to jump through the ridiculous hoops you put in place to keep you all in a job - moreover its a job which contributes nothing to the economy and does absolutely nothing to contribute the sum total of human happiness - rather the opposite.......

Man at desk: Here is the address of the service des mines. Next please.

Me: Thank you for your time and kind advice.

Scene 8 The Service des Mines at Rivesaltes - two weeks later

Maggie: Here is the car for inspection.

Mechanic: It's a Honda Civic.

Maggie: Yes, here's the *certificat de conformité.*

Mechanic: OK (signs certificate)

Maggie: But don't you need to examine the car?

Mechanic: No Madame I can see that it is a Honda Civic.

Maggie: Thank you for your time and kind advice.

Scene 9: The *Préfecture* at Perpignan. the following week.

Man at desk:.You seem to have all the papers now, monsieur, here is the *Carte Grise.* That will be 80 euros.

We: Hallelujah. Praise be to the Prefect by whom all things are possible. (Exeunt all)

Grande Finale (all characters appear on stage singing and high-kicking)

All: Bureaucracy, bureaucracy, there's nothing in the world can beat bureaucracy
Sous prefet: If you wonder what you're at
Taxman: Or you want to pay your VAT
All: You'll find it all intact in our bureaucracy

All: Bureaucracy, bureaucracy, unemployment would be worse without bureaucracy
Lady prefecture: Though it makes you want to sob
Mechanic: It will keep us in a job
All: And you can shut your bleeding gob about bureaucracy

All: Bureaucracy, bureaucracy, we are prisoners of the system of bureaucracy

Control Technique Lady: It's the way we keep control
Mayor's Secretary: Of your body and your soul
All: And we've got you pigeon-holed in our bureaucracy

All: Bureaucracy, bureaucracy there's never any doubt about
bureaucracy
Insurance Agent: If you want a new *Carte Grise*
Man at prefet: We make you buckle at the knees
All: It costs the earth to please us all, bureau-crac-y

FIN

Now that we had become the proud owners of a French-registered
car, it was only a moment, and another 40 euros, to have the new
plates forged and fitted. We looked in pride at our new *plaques
d'immatriculation*. We had taken a financial and temporal beating
from the system, but in a sense we had beaten it too, mostly by
perseverance. At the very least we had survived it. Or so we
thought. Two months later the engine blew up and we had to buy
another car. This time we played safe. We bought a Citroen. The
blighters had won after all.

We could also dwell on the contortions we had to endure before
our *Carte de Séjour* arrived through our letter box almost exactly
one year later after being referred back 5 times for evidence of
health insurance, eligibility for old age pension, copies of birth,
marriage, and vocational pension certificates translated by
authorised and registered French fonctionnaires, Maggie's and
my mothers' maiden names, when, where and how often we blew
our noses during the day, great grandmother's toilet habits etc etc
and.....

But hold on one little minute! No-one forced us to come to live in
France. We made the decision, as in marriage, for better or for
worse, in sickness and in health, on the settee or in bed, and we
accepted that this was a complete package - good and bad, light
and dark, Laurel and Hardy, rain and shine, Mutt and Jeff. It's a
new culture, and no matter that the French themselves don't like
the bureaucracy any more than we do, we chose to live here with
our eyes wide open. So we have the odd spat with unreasonable

authority or the lady behind the counter who would rather chat to the customer in front than serve us!. Who doesn't have these sort of hassles in any new country? It's part of the examination system.

Moving to another culture might be described as a test of character. It might also be described as a novel form of self-flagellation or a way of filling in the entry papers for the lunatic asylum. It depends who you are, and how much you want to keep the mind open and stimulated. For us, it has a hundred more plusses than minuses and the challenge keeps our mental juices in jacuzzi order. Certainly we feel that, in our many moves during a working lifetime and especially in this one, probably our last before the man with the scythe gives one or other of us the final push, we have enriched our lives beyond measure.

The many good colleagues and friends we have made from all nationalities have shown, to our satisfaction at least, that national stereotypes are exactly that - stereotypes with little basis in reality. We have met, befriended, dined with and come to love popular oxymorons like intellectual Americans, moderate and secular Arabs, industrious Africans, merry Japanese, highly-strung Australians, humble Frenchmen and gourmand Germans, happy Indians - very few nationalities we have met and mingled with fit the archetypes we were both conditioned to believe when young.

They survive only through today's media. We have, through them, learned to respect their cultures and we have found in every case more than enough common ground to make for lively conversation and fruitful debate. Many times and in many parts of the world, we have, with our foreign friends, discussed and solved the problems of man's inhumanity to man. They have helped us to become more mature people. They will always remain a part of us. More than that we hope that we are a part of them and this can only be good for understanding and tolerance in a world somewhat light on those characteristics.

Our professorial friend Mike and Josie, his wife, live in Clara. They too have moved quite frequently during an academic lifetime and lived in Wales, California, Germany, Scotland and now the

Conflent. Their grandson was one of the children at Dunblane who did not attend school on that fateful day in April 1992, and the closeness of the miss still haunts them. They too need the stimulus of a changing culture fix and they too have an open outlook on most topics. Mike's language skills are much greater than ours, as befits a semiologist, and so is his knowledge of the law. He is prepared to go to war with the more intransigent bureaucratic officials in the same way that the French do. Mike is also an acuminate observer of the human condition in the Conflent and author of the excellent 'Letters from French Catalonia.'

Also a great raconteur, he sometimes relates the story of his battle with authority in the matter of linguistics. In order to obtain some of the benefits of living in France an *etranger* has to prove that his or her visible corporeal body has an official existence in the real world by producing an official translation of the birth certificate, and that spouses are indeed spouses by a translation of the marriage certificate - there are tax benefits for that. The fluent foreign French speaker and writer is not allowed to do this himself no matter how erudite and articulate in the language - oh no - it has to be done word by word by an officially recognised translator recognised by the state and licensed to give it, literally, the stamp of authority.

The list of such people is quite small in many areas and of course, most of them already keep a standard translation in their computers and so do no more than insert the new name. They charge the earth for this privilege. It's a racket of course and France is not the only European country to condone it - Britain and Germany are two more who play this game on unsuspecting newcomers.

Mike, as I have said is a world-class semiologist - his trade is words in whatever language. He has spent 20 years as a Professor of Languages in several universities in Germany, USA and the United Kingdom and was a Vice-President of the Institute of Linguists. His knowledge of the French language comes with a guarantee and a silver tongue, better than the French, and he knows far more about translation than most translators. So of course he did his own interpretations. But come the inevitable time when these had to be presented to officialdom without the magic stamp, so came the inevitable rejection. Mike was not so easily defeated, nor did he believe that there is any substance in law which would establish the inferiority of his own translation against that of the language mafia. He confronted the Mayor and was told that it was none of his affair - the *préfecture* made the decisions. He confronted the official at the *préfecture* and in flawless French told him the position, then his position and background and proved why his translation was not only accurate but also more authentic since the standard translation had made several common linguistic errors.

The luckless *fonctionnaire* promised to take his complaint to higher authority. This in itself is a minor triumph since French civil servants are highly trained to wither with a twitch of an eyebrow anyone who dares to question authority. Meanwhile Mike, determined if not foolhardy, has engaged the support of his colleagues in the French Institute of Linguistics and solicited their confirmation of his points and passed these on to the office. Three years later, the case is still sub judice. The *préfecture* has not deigned to reply, nor will it probably. Mike is considering whether to continue with the crusade and risk raising further his already high blood pressure, or abandon it in the interests of a quiet life, which is the fervent hope of all bureaucracies everywhere.

Tales of the Conflent

Chapter the Fourth

The Touryst Guyde's Tale

Part 1 - Your Handbook to Paradyse

**Being the tale of how a simple Catalan girl can
bring places in Paradise to life**

The Tourist Guide's Tale

Hullo. My name is Naomi and I am your guide to this, the most beautiful place in France, in Europe, in the world. Well, maybe I'm biased but my continuing salary depends on my persuading you of the truth of it. Not that you will need much persuading, since the beautiful Conflent can tell its own tale of spectacular views, magnificent towns and villages, majestic mountains and lovable people – well, some of them. Like me for instance. And as for the whiff of history! My goodness, we have more resources than a politician's expense account on that score. The whole Conflent reeks of it. So, rather than listening to me wittering on like a parrot on steroids, let's get started on what some insect group in England called a magical mystery tour. That was all before my time and I haven't a clue what they were on about but it's true that there is a large dollop of magic, but for me not a lot of mystery. It's just mother nature in her most colourful clothes.

I understand that the Ymmygrant, pretentious idiot, has warbled profusely on about the Conflent villages in the first of these tales. So, although I could do a much better job than he did, I'll start with the towns, the places you are most likely to find yourselves in when you finally set foot in this demi-heaven. There are no cities in the Conflent. The nearest is Perpignan, some forty kilometres away, and that's where we sometimes go for a little night-life. Not that there's much of that there either if it's clubbing you're after. Closing time would be around 9 pm and after that what you get up to is done in the comfort of your own homes. Anyway, back to the glorious Conflent. Our major metropolises boast a population of about six thousand souls and are more like larger villages, the focus for markets, shopping and other sundry activities that take a peasant's fancy. I won't elaborate on what some of those might be, but, as the ymmygrant said, our summer nightlife can get pretty hectic. We'll start the tour with my own home town of Prades, pearl of the valley.

Prades

My town of Prades is the regional capital of the Conflent. It finds itself itself plumb in the centre of the region just where the valley of the Tet begins its climb into the high Pyrennees. It's a pretty town, though Mr Michelin did not see fit to give it even one star in his celebrated green guides. Maybe it's because it has the feeling and smell of a busy working community and he got a bit sniffy about that. But the views from the town centre are real enough. In the snow-filled winter, the Canigou seems to rise abruptly out of the Southern outskirts of the town like a majestic nine-thousand foot high cream-cake. And on its Western and Northern sides the peaks of the Lower Pyrennees and the Fenouilledes answer defiantly back.

Prades – music time

For a town so squeezed in a magnificent monster mountain garlic crusher Prades could not be more serene. It's so laid back that people walking the streets after 8 pm are considered to be peculiar, mad or up to no good. Just joking of course, but sometimes even I often wonder if the place has become a ghost town.

But this is usually during the winter somnolence. After that's over, the town springs and summers into life as if to make up for all that inactivity. It bubbles like a discontented geyser. To feel the sheer frenetic ambience of the place, you should visit on a Tuesday morning, when the two squares and the surrounding streets dance and resonate to the frantic bustle and chatter of the weekly market. Here you will be able to sample, there and then, the culinary delights that set the stomach in motion and the appetite into freefall - chorizos from South America, subtle delicacies from the South Seas, *boles de Picolat*, spicy meat balls in a tangy sauce, and, this being Catalonia, a truly giant paella from which gourmands like you can savour a pan-lid full of crustaces, chicken and saffron rice.

Should you wish to delay these pleasures of the table, there are the joys of the palate to be transported home - cheeses of every variety including the delicious Pyrennean Manchego and Etorki, cheeses from cow, sheep and goat, cheeses hard as iron, cheeses soft as fleece and cheeses in colours and states of a viscosity unseen in British markets. In the summer, it's one of my weekly diversions to watch bemused Brits circulate the stands with perplexed expressions, as if suffering from shell-shock. Their olfactory senses are being invaded by odours they have rarely experienced, and their brains are overwhelmed by the diversity.

The full array of stalls is bewildering for the unsuspecting grockel. One of them appeals solely to the connoisseur of prunes and displays several varieties of this very useful working fruit. Many customers for this product tend to be well advanced in years. Another stand will pander to the olive fanatic, tens of different olives in tens of different dressings, bland and piquant, black and green, large and tiny, laurel and hardy; yet another will concentrate on mushrooms, cepes, girolles, the delicious chanterelles and the sinister sounding *trompettes de la mort*, each separate variety destined for a different dish. My Catalan friends and neighbours know their cuisine.

Part of the Plane-tree covered Prades market

And of course there are the products of the region, fruits of every kind, vegetables of every persuasion, wines of every strength and sausages of every content. The Prades market is a truly happy and animated affair - musicians abound, accordionists, violinists, trumpeters, guitarists, saxophonists and more. One of them even plays the triangle. Together it is a symphony of sound - and a magnet for people from all the villages of the Conflent and beyond. In summer the whole scene resembles one of USAP's more violent rugby scrums - pushing, pulling, scratching, fighting and the odd touch of eye-gouging when the referee isn't looking.

After the market it is chattering time. The *étrangers* gather in the *Café de France* to exchange the vital news and gossip of the week. How Martha's toenails were cut last Thursday, Bill's gout is getting worse, and what a worry Marjorie's cataracts have turned out to be. By contrast, the local people hurry home to cook and devour a large *déjeuner* followed by an even larger siesta - no

Catalan worth his salt will be found out in the streets between the
hours of twelve and three.

Well it so happens that the Ymmygrant. The pretentious guy who
wrote the first chapter of this book also wrote a poem about
Prades market and I'm sure he's be gnashing his teeth if I didn't
print it here/ So here goes

Prades Market

Each Tuesday all year, Prades moves into gear
It's market day in the town square
Hundreds of stalls entice and enthrall
The whole of the Conflent is there

The old marketplace frees up all its space
For the colourful, bustling occasion
The market spreads down through the east part of town
A peaceful commercial invasion

There's cheeses perchance from all parts of France
And some from the neighbouring lands
Roquefort, Vacherin and Tomme Catalan
A hundred and one different brands

Mushrooms light your fire? Fill you with desire ?
There's a stall that will make your heart soar
Girolles, chanterelles, pleurotes, coulemelles
And delicious trompettes de la mort

Or perhaps it's the prune that makes your mind swoon
To relieve your routine constipation
There's a man who imports 7 different sorts
For a colon -inspired liberation

Want something to eat ? Savoury or Sweet
Everyone gets their own wish
See that old fellah who's buying Paella
He comes every week for the fish.

There's veggies and fruit and something to suit

All tastes, all crazes, all needs
Live music abounds, a concerto of sounds
In harmonious rhythms and speeds

What about clothes ? You'll appreciate those
The range is beyond comprehension
All sizes and shapes from dresses to capes
And prices for those on a pension

The brits are among the bustling throng
They gather together in gangs
At closure they dine, consume lots of wine
And go home with head-bells that clang

So get thee along with a skip and a song
To the pride of the Conflentais towns
You'll be certain to buy without knowing why
And before the market shuts down

We'll say it again, just come about ten
If it's perfect fulfilment you seek
Don't come at one, for everyone's gone
And Prades sleeps again for a week

©The YmmYgrant

Neat Huh?. Well I like it.

The Prades Retable

My pride and joy is Prade's major claim to fame, Its church boasts
the largest baroque *retable,* or altar-screen, in Europe - not the
most beautiful, the most ornate or the most intricate, but the
largest. And indeed for me, and for you, it is a wondrous sight.
Those of you who are historians will know that back in post-
Reformation times, in the 16th century, the Pope and the Holy
Roman Emperor were preparing to rescue their flocks from the
opposing protestant product.

And so they convened an Executive Task Force of bishops and called it the Council of Trent. It was given the mission of developing a counter-reformation marketing plan that would blast the protestant competition out of the water, and return the lost sheep into the catholic fold.

Recognising that one of the barriers might be the fact that no-one could understand latin, except maybe the priest, and even that wasn't certain, one of its many recommendations, as the leaflet in the church says in impeccable English, was to produce clear, coherent and realistic Art, at least that's what it says on the promotional packet. This strategy, it was supposed, would enable the faithful to learn the truth and wisdom of the bible stories and restore them to the catholic paths of righteousness. The expert sculptors of baroque retables, or altar-pieces, in the Conflent were thus a kind of holy salesman, marketing their product much as the towns butchers purveyed their meat, and the farriers their horseshoes.

The Prades Retable in the church of St Pierre

So back to the *retable*. It's right at the front, and the investment of one euro into the box on the left will illuminate it in all its glory for five minutes. So what's on this masterwork from the past? Since the Prades church is dedicated to St Pierre it isn't surprising that the centre piece of the altar-piece depicts a life-size St Peter, the patron Saint of the church and first pope. He's surrounded by six major events in the biblical story of his life – in temporal order, his calling as a disciple, the giving of the keys, the deliverance, the miracle at the Golden Gate, St Peter walking on the water and his crucifixion.

Not an insignificant list of experiences, and enough real meat there, one would have thought, for the devout non-latin speaker to sit in quiet contemplation for a whole morning's service, while the Curé droned forth in a language they didn't understand. But such meagre fare was not for the Sunyer brothers, who came from Manresa in Spain to demonstrate their extraordinary carpentry skills. This was only the hors d'œuvres. As an amuse-gueule between courses so to speak, or perhaps between the first lesson and the sermon, sundry other disciples make a guest appearance on Peter's left - Saints Simon, James and Paul and these are equally balanced by Jude, Philip and Andrew on the right, a true galaxy of divine stars.

Now the faithful, my ancestors remember, really do have enough to occupy their mind during the long winter devotions, one would think. But I'm afraid not, the brothers really also wanted to confirm that this is no ordinary register of biblical characters and so, as a side plate, the fathers of the doctrine - Jerome, Gregory, Augustine and Ambrose - join the caste as corroboration that this is really serious stuff.

And just in case the point had not yet been driven home and to maintain unbroken, undiminished interest, the temporal and spiritual position of St Peter in the general hierarchy of things is depicted as a main course by carving the Virgin of the immaculate conception above him with all power coming from God the Father and the Holy Spirit above her. Attendant angels are thrown in for good measure as dessert.

I hope that you are all still with me on this tour of this remarkable retable – I suspect that, for the barbarian mind, the minutiae of 17th century religious fervour might be a new intellectual experience, rather like reading a manual on carpet-laying for dummies. But there will be a test at the end and those who fail will be required to read the full liturgical repertoire from beginning to end - just joking, of course. But just ponder on how all of this provided the pious 17th century believer with enough reverential material to last the whole week until the next visit.

It did the trick and that is all that mattered for them, and for the church too, much as the advertising of Kellogg's Rice Krispies maintains its customer base. Even to this day, when latin has been excommunicated from the liturgy, it relieves the sometimes dreary hours spent by ex-patriate Catholic Britons in listening to long sermons delivered in furious French like a series of Gilbert and Sullivan patter songs. The reason is often that the priest has another service to get to after this one, and neither the sound system nor the acoustics are good enough to allow one word to be distinguished from the next.

If this description sounds a little irreverent it is not intended to be so. After all I was brought up to be a devout catholic myself. These Conflent altar-pieces are remarkably clear, coherent, lavish and often dramatic. They are also in most cases sumptuously coloured, even through the accumulated dust of centuries, and they perform the task for which they were created perfectly. Ornamental masons and carpenters were in great demand in the 16th and 17th centuries and would often spend as much as a year creating a piece for a particular church.

The *retable* in the Prades church is not alone. They are a major feature of almost every church of any size in the whole area and the more intellectual visitors could do worse, if they are so inclined, than to spend a complete holiday visiting the holy places to compare *retables*. As a start I can recommend the churches in Villefranche, Ille-sur-Têt, Eus, Collioure, Vinça and Espira de Conflent, each of them different in size, story and impact. In their domination they sometimes dwarf other equally interesting treasures. At Prade's St Pierre, the most beautiful sculptural work is not in fact the *retable* but a 16th century crucifixion piece called the Black Christ, which comes with an unhappy legend attached to it.

Folklore has it that every time the Black Christ leaves the church a priest dies and, as with many legends, it has a basis in experience. Once, in a time of drought, it was taken around the boundaries of the town to encourage the arrival of rain. Within the month one of the three priests who carried it was dead. And that wasn't the first time this had happened. So it isn't perhaps surprising that the effigy hasn't been outside the church for many years, though the reason, according to the church authorities, has more to do with the burden of its great weight on the heart than with any fear of malediction.

Climbing the Canigou

And so we come to Prades third most important claim to fame, some would say the real reason for visiting. Our town is also the gateway to the Canigou, the sacred mountain of us Catalans. The mountain dominates its streets, its people and its economy, rather as a big hole in the ground governs the lives of the inhabitants of Padirac in the Dordogne or, as I am told, black puddings in the marketplaces of Bury in England. In the summer, fleets of jeeps leave the surrounding villages like speedy camel caravans to transport eager-faced tourists like you up to the Chalet des Cortalets, a refuge two thirds up the mountain, from whence it is possible to trudge the remaining 3000 feet to its summit. And a trudge it certainly is.

Some years ago I visited Scotland and climbed the UK's highest mountain, Ben Nevis - just half the height of the Canigou, I might add. Those who have slogged that path up Ben Nevis will be familiar with the syndrome. Around every next bend, one expects to see the end of the agony. And around every next bend there is another bend, until, after several hours of agonising anticipation, the sudden appearance of the actual summit cairn comes as a disappointing anti-climax.

The trudge to the Canigou summit

The Canigou is no different for the majority of its ascent. The first flush of enthusiasm sees brave grockels start out on a serpentine path that meanders upward ever upward and ever steeper with the intention of showing to their friends back home how easy this mountaineering can be and returning as conquering heroes. Many of these idiots are dressed for a party, in anything from sandals to winkle-pickers to high-heeled gucchi shoes. Bare-chested machos vie with flimsy silk singlets to challenge the unpredictable might of the mountain. The average fitness level would make a couch-potato look like an Olympic athlete. As they climb higher, their progress becomes ever more laboured and breathless. Many fall by the wayside and stagger, pooped and shattered, down to the less demanding comforts of the chalet bar, where they exchange harrowing tales of great bravery and fortitude on the mountain. Those who persevere sometimes reach a level 600 feet below the peak. From there they have to scramble desperately and inelegantly over a tricky shattered and weathered rock pile. I'm told that Great Gable in the English Lake District offers a similar examination of balance, judgement and determination, though at a considerably lower height.

Mission accomplished – stupendous views

On their triumphant arrival at its zenith, they discover that the zephyr that was blowing gently through the streets of the town below has transmuted into a howling tempest and that the temperature has mysteriously fallen by some 20 degrees. How unreasonable of the mountain. The party is off. Most don't linger to admire the magnificent views in all directions from, weather permitting, Barcelona in the South to Montpellier in the West and Toulouse in the North. And, of course, of the tiny ant colony of Prades below, whence they came. A few huddle and shiver pitifully behind the rusting iron cross that some heroic climbers lugged up and erected in the late 1800s.

But it offers neither warmth nor succour, and they quickly realise that the only way is down, and down a considerable distance for their already aching limbs. And so, knees trembling with effort and muscles screaming with pain they hobble down to the refuge to join their now well plastered friends on the transport back to Prades. That happens every day in the three months of Summer when the sun shines and the snow has diminished to a few dirty white patches under the north-facing rocks. From late September the mountain replenishes its icy defences and becomes out of bounds to all but the most intrepid alpine climbers.

Villefranche de Conflent. Guardian of the People

But of course Prades and the Canigou aren't the only the starting point for an exploration of this magic paradise. Just up the valley lies the UNESCO World Heritage site of Villefranche de Conflent. But first, I'm afraid that you may have to endure the boredom of another little history lesson. There will be no examination but you are expected to apply what you learn here into your daily life. Just joking again. Remember I said earlier that we are rolling in this historical stuff. If I had been born 500 and more years ago I would not have been French.

This land has experienced a rich and chequered history, having at any one time been a part of the Balearics, Catalonia, Aragon, Spain and, only in the last 450 years, France. Those of you who have read your maps may have noticed that many of the village names, Belesta, Pézilla etc - are succeeded by the words 'de la frontière'. One can trace the old frontier line between France and Spain in this way. The old Saracen fort at Salses near Perpignan still marks the extreme eastern reach of the Spanish Moors, who influenced the region many years ago, and in Perpignan itself there is the *Palais des Rois de Majorque* to remind us of the years of Balearic power.

It was Louis XIV who settled it all. As one of life's 17th century megalomaniacs, similar to the 20th century's Hitler, Stalin, Mao and Thatcher (just joking with the last, of course – or am I?), he was of course always right – even when he was wrong. He wanted his country to have its natural boundaries – the Rhine in the East, la Manche to the North, the Atlantic in the West and the Pyrennees in the South West, and he had the military resources to jolly well make sure it happened. After a particularly bad spell of gout, this little piece of Spain where we now stand, on what he considered to be his side of the Pyrennees, niggled him and he lusted after rectifying the anomale. (This was not the only thing the Sun King lusted after, as Madame de Maintenon and many others would testify if they were still alive and kicking so to speak – but that's not relevant to this story).

So he sent an army, which duly defeated the Spaniards. The result was the Treaty of the Pyrennees, signed in 1659, to establish the line of the high mountains as the natural frontier. He also grabbed half of the Cerdagne, a hanging valley 40 kilometres into the mountains, for France, with the exception of the peculiar Spanish enclave of Llivia, an unusual piece of land entirely surrounded by French territory. The remains of his conquest can be seen in the magnificent fortresses, built by a geezer called Vauban. Vauban was Louis' military building foreman, a sort of territory fixer. If Louis wanted a fortress building, he was the guy to whom he would turn.

He was especially good at ramparts, seeing them as essential to the safety of the townspeople of the day. And so it was in the 1660s, The Spaniards were not, as can be expected, exactly happy bunnies about the loss of the territory they had held for thousands of years, and some of the more hot-headed of them would make sorties into the new France to pillage and plunder. This is where Vauban comes in. Louis, who had a fairly short fuse where land was involved, would turn to him and say 'Those damned Spaniards are making trouble, please fix it Mr Vauban', though history does not record if he used the word please. Indeed it is unlikely that this is so. Whatever the result was the afore-mentioned impregnables, one called Mont Louis at the Western gateway to the Cerdagne, and the other just up the road from Prades.

And that Ladies and gentlemen brings us to the, I say it again in case you have had a memory lapse, UNESCO World heritage site of Villefranche de Conflent. It stands sentinel, an urban guardsman, at a magnificent site at the confluence of the Cadi and Têt valleys just before they emerge on to the plain and where it is narrow enough to make sure that no-one with nefarious intent, or maybe too much money, passes by. Mountains rise precipitously above it on every side. Perversely, and in keeping with the manners and mores of our time, it is now, 350 years later, grockelsville, the tourist trap to end all tourist traps. And quite justifiably so. Its houses retain the character of its greatest triumph such that the ghosts of the people who lived at the time can be felt in their stones. Not in summertime though - the place is yet another rugby scrum of constantly milling humanity.

Villefranche de Conflent – A UNESCO World Heritage Site

Perceptive visitors will find a basically 2-street town restored to its 17th century image, or at least to the image which that imaginative French restorer of the 19th century, Viollet-le Duc, supposed it ought to have been. That guy had a real feeling for what 20th and 21st century tourists want to see. They may wish to browse in the wall-to-wall tourist shops, tastefully hidden in the ground floors of the houses, selling leather goods, ceramics, home made wooden toys, bars of soap, 21st century antiques, Zorro shirts, Kellogg's Frosties, paintings, fossils, candles - all of surprisingly good quality for an exploiter's paradise. They will not see unsightly advertising since that is rigidly controlled. After buying ice-creams for the kids, they can, for the payment of a small fee, visit and tour the impressive ramparts which surround three sides of the town

For an even smaller fee they can climb the thousand steps inside the adjoining mountain to visit Fort Liberia, a garrison perched high above the town in a gesture of protection. Or, a thousand steps being potential heart attack material, they may wish to ascend by the navette or by horse, neither of which mount the steps, but find a more congenial way of reaching the top. From there they will see how the fort controls the view to East, West and South, experience the gruesome remains of its life as a 19th century prison, pretend to be a 17th century general and perhaps invest in another ice-cream.

At this point it is decision time. To descend by the tunnel staircase (which should be infinitely preferable to ascending it), or to return on the rattletrap which brought them here in the first place. Many decide on the first option. Half-way down, too late, they realise their mistake. Once again, knees trembling and muscles screaming for mercy they wonder how they will complete the descent. But the human spirit always prevails and arrive they do, making their stiff-legged way to the nearest bar for a recuperative drink. Those who are still able may wish to visit the ancient and beautiful church of St Jacques, look at the beautiful 14th century lifesize wooden carving of a recumbent Christ, carried around the town at Easter time, and the *retable*, also a work of Sunyer.

On entering they could not miss the beautiful pink marble portal which affords both entrance and egress. Outside the church in the town's main square, the Auberge St Michel would be delighted to help slake their thirst and the Auberge St Paul assuage their hunger. The latter has a reputation which extends well beyond the region but it is as well to carry a capacious purse if one chooses this option. And expect to have to top up with more ice creams since this is a nouvelle cuisine establishment. Burly British stevedores and well-endowed lady gourmets are well advised to avoid this option, as are those who earn less than the average merchant banker.

Leaving the charm and bustle of the town and climbing the hill across the road a little way, visitors can transform themselves into speleologists by visiting the caves of Les Canalettes. They were discovered relatively recently in 1931 and contain some of the most interesting stalactite, stalagmite and eccentric formations to be found in France. The grand cavern right in the centre of the mountain is particularly capacious and beautiful. Besides the shimmering white pillars and the pendulous grandeur of the stalactites, its roof is covered by tiny white three inch long udders of glistening calcium carbonate as if a thousand cows had combined to create an enormous extended bovine chandelier.

Spectacular views in the depths of the mountain

If the visitor chooses to go caving in the evening, he/she may be fortunate enough to experience the *Son et Lumière*. For this, the cavern is converted into a large theatrical auditorium. It is rather like sitting in an enormous womb, one with enormous polyps as if it were potentially carcinogenic. The musical pageant starts with an *hors d'oeuvres variés* by a visiting choir. Even the famous Eus Chorale, described in the Choir Leader's tale, has sounded very good here, the acoustics, if not the voices, being nigh on perfect. For the main course however, the lights are extinguished and darkness envelopes the auditorium, a thick, black, velvet absence of light, such as can only be experienced in the middle of mountains.

Judiciously hidden loud speakers, high on channel wattage and resonating through the blackness, strike up the opening bars of Richard Strauss's famous '*Also Sprach Zarathrustra*' and the coloured lights slowly awake. It is corny, it is clichéed, it is deafening and it sure is effective. As a celebration of humankind's genius this triumphal tone poem takes some beating, and here in this lonely cave it shatters the silence and refashions the imagination. As the decibels rise, one half expects to see the tiny chandelier stalactites come hurtling down to strike everyone in the audience dead, but fortunately they stay where they have been for the last thousand centuries. The Strauss fades out and other selections of music, classical, popular, strings, voice, orchestral, big band, quintet fade in

A troop of Cossack horsemen singing just like the Red Army Choir start their journey faintly from the depths of the cavern behind, rise slowly to a crescendo of clopping feet and ghostly melodious male voices as they ride invisibly through the chamber where the open-mouthed grockels sit, and fall again to a barely perceptible diminuendo as they disappear down the exit tunnel to the cave entrance. Meanwhile, lights of all colours illuminate the grotesque geological structures and dance in a phantasmagoria of radiance and shadow, while attempting to mirror the warmth and tonal features of the music.

Pavarotti never sounded, nor looked, like this before and nor did Robbie Williams. It is all very well done and calculated to please every audience. As the punters evacuate the claustrophobic core of the mountain in search of the red army ghosts at the end of the performance, the excited chatter along the wooden walkways reveals that the cave's rich promise has been eminently fulfilled. Opposite the dark entrance to the cave, the welcoming lights of Villefranche propose more fleshly comforts to supplement the elation of mind and spirit. But the Cossacks are nowhere to be seen – they have moved on into the night.

Before we say goodbye to the charms of Villefranche, I have another treat for you. Wouldn't you know it but that bloody Ymmigrant wrote a poem about that too. I'd better let you see it or he'll throw a hissy fit. So here goes. It's a bit corny in places but at least he tried.

Villefranche Mon Amour.

Deep in the valleys where Cady meets Tet
Guarding the passage where all roads must meet
You'll find a rare jewel you''ll never forget
Villefranche de Conflent's mediaeval seat

In the year sixteen hundred and fifty nine
King Louis fourteenth forced a treaty with Spain
To confirm the border and define the line
Behind which the Spanish should ever remain

He sent his chief engineer, Vauban by name
To protect his new subjects from retaliation
His fervent endeavour and primary aim
To seal his domains by fortification

Vauban constructed a fortress of stone
Patrolled by soldiers by day and by night
It stands to this day but is now better known
As a noted UNESCO World heritage site

Strong rock-hard ramparts seem to hold power
Over the two ancient streets of the town
Further improved by fortified towers
To give early warning and close a threat down

Enter Villefranche by an impressive gate
Into the world of the late middle age

Then let your creative mind liberate
Yourself from its twenty-first century cage

A town where pink marble is everywhere found
On porticos, sidewalks, churches and walls
It permeates all the buildings around
With a pink glow where the morning light falls

Wander the many commercial spaces
Watch modern craftsmen create old from new
Dine at the many gourmandise places
All with a terrace and exquisite view

Enter the church through the low sunken doorway
Note the asymmetry caused by two naves
Rare sacred art where the rich and the poor pray
Fine Roman capitals and carved architraves

Follow the legend of Villefranche's witches
Who pass the winter in caverns nearby
Bringing good luck and the promise of riches
By casting their spells when springtime is nigh

Time to explore Fort Liberia's showplace
High on the mountain above the old town
Access by subterranean staircase
A thousand steps up, the same coming down

Garrison, barracks, dungeon and prison
Its scope and its history is stirring and vast
Well-informed guides will expand the vision
Of stories and people in centuries past

Back in the township that Vauban enhanced
Wander the ramparts where his footsteps strode
Imagine the scene and become entranced
Savour the birthright your forebears bestowed

If there is still time you must not forget
To cross the main road with intent to explore

The impressive cave of the Grandes Canalettes
A journey into the mountain's deep core

Stalactities, stalagmites, pillars and sinks
A vast darkened chamber where music is played
A view of pre-history to entice us to think
How progress through time is mostly man-made.

A day in Villefranche is a memory for life
One that will remain with you forever
Where you discover how conflict and strife
Cen be overcome by human endeavour
©Norman Longworth

Now you may think that the places I have already described would
be enough for a super sight-seeing holiday in the sun. I expect
that you have already been down to the travel agent to enquire
about how to get here. You would of course be right to do so. But
there is more – much more. The Conflent is nothing if it doesn't
have variety to offer. For that though you will need to move on to
the second part of my Tourist Guide's tale. Happy Reading

Naomi

TALES OF THE CONFLENT

Chapter the Fyfth

The Touryst Guyde's Tale

Part 2: Strangers yn Paradyse

Being the continuing tale of one of the world's most beautiful regions

The Tourist Guide's Tale part 2

Here I am again. Naomi, you recall. I wrote the first Tourist Guide Tale. I expect that your tickets will have arrived by now. So I am going to tickle up your appetite with yet more of the sights of this earthly Conflent paradise. You won't be bored I assure you. So here we go. Let's start with the place where the Brits of yesteryear congregated.

Vernet les Bains. The story of a church and more.

Driving up from the Vaubanian stronghold of Villefranche, past the caves and the less than noteworthy village of Corneilla, the discerning driver will come to a small town. On the right, rising up above a distinctly rocky river, there appears into view a somewhat non-descript building with the words 'LES THERMES' writ large on its Northern Wall. This is the clue to where we now are.

Vernet-les Bains is, as its name suggests, a spa town. It finds itself on the slopes of the Canigou often wondering why it is so much colder up there than in the Conflent valley below. But it has a rather special history going back into the dark ages. The locals had always known that their water had healing qualities. If they had warts or piles or had been a bit heavy on the mead the previous evening, they would pop up the road for mug of mountain-fresh hot spring water and after a few days all would be well again healthwise. I

n medieval times, the monks from the Abbey of St Martin nearby were the unchallenged owners of the spring, and they used it as a marketing tool for their own brand label of feudal Christianity. A sort of 'drink our water and feel the spirit – it's holier than the competition at Molitg across the valley' campaign. This lasted unchanged for centuries until the Vernet populace gradually cottoned on to the dodge, or improved communications enabled them to cross the valley to Molitg to test the hypothesis. A neat case of travel broadening the mind.

But it is this water, and the medical infrastructure built up around it, that is the source of the town's prosperity. Over the centuries the number of sources multiplied from one to many and the size of the buildings around them escalated from a stone hut to a facility which offers 100s of patients swimming pools, personal bathtubs, over and under-water massage (one hesitates to guess what the latter actually entailed), steam rooms, seated bathing and pulverisation chambers (this last possibly cribbed from the Gestapo manual when they were operating in the region during the second world war). The progenitor of this expansion was a 19th century rich banker (what else), who also funded the provision of hotels, doctors , attendants and tender loving care. The rich and famous flocked to the sanatorium for their daily dose of health-giving torture. Inevitably, the venture was a great success and the banker became, as bankers do, even richer.

Vernet is also the only place in France with a monument to celebrate the 1904 Entente Cordiale, which is precisely one more than there is in the rest of Europe, including the UK, thus demonstrating a) the extent of the knowledge of the treaty among the peoples of France and Britain at the time and/or b) its ability to grab their imaginations as an event worth commemorating. More about this later.

 Vernet's heyday was in the years before and after the turn of the 20th century. English Lords and Ladies, Minor and Major Royals, retired Generals and wealthy and impecunious poets descended annually to the town winter and summer, mostly the former. It became an outpost of the British Empire where the sun never sets and the natives know their place, and are eternally grateful for having it frequently pointed out to them. Forelock time in the sun.

During the day the thermal springs would dispense hope and hot salty water to the aristocratic guests, and in the evening the tables of the Vernet Casino would dispense with their considerable proportion of the then British Gross National Product. This was a time of great optimism and prosperity, for the visitors at least. La Belle Epoch, when ladies bustled through the town in colourful costumes and carried gaudy parasols and the men wore bowler hats and prominent moustaches. The town basked in a riot of confidence and cheerfulness.

Into this hedonistic, pleasure-seeking milieu, like the intellectual cavalry, rode the writer and poet, Rudyard Kipling, he of the jungle book and despatches from India. His wife, Carrie, was stricken with arthritis and a Swiss Medicine man had recommended the sulphurous waters of Vernet les Bains as the best cure. The great man moved in exalted circles for a humble journalist from India. It was a time when poets were revered rather than reviled, especially among the fading political intelligentsia, the military has-beens and the outer royalty who frequented Vernet. Kipling's moustache was in great demand at the soirées of the period, since it danced gracefully while reciting his poetry and transcended the moustaches of the other eminent Edwardians in the audience.

But he certainly had an effect on the French. Although he never inhabited Vernet permanently, his influence is indelibly imprinted upon the urban psyche of the town. Until recently there was an annual Kipling Festival, when every nook and cranny that the luminary visited would be celebrated in both song and word. Today he would have a tour manager, a gaggle of roadies, a fleet of publicity experts and a decibel-rich panoply of high fidelity loudspeakers.

He would be a star celebrity and invited to eat wichity grubs in the outback of Australia. Which perhaps says more about the brash excesses of the modern age than it does about the elegant respectability of the pre-world-war 1 era. Because of his influence, the local Council has not yet considered whether to rename the town Kipling les Bains, but its economy has owed a hefty slice of its income to his name. That this is diminishing is probably due to the fact that most of Europe and three quarters of the modern-day Brits who come here believe that the Jungle book was written by Walt Disney, and that Kipling is a baker who markets cakes and buns.

The case of the lost church

It was a time when, if anything typically British was in short supply, it would be provided by subscription from the wealthy visitors. The afore-mentioned unique 1904 monument to the Entente Cordiale is one rather strange example. Another is St Georges Church. They were having nothing of the Catholic hegemony in their town. Anglicanism was a glaring omission from the cultural and religious landscape, and by jove and Lord Roberts, it would be rectified. Princess Beatrice of Battenberg (the royal not the cake – and not baked by Mr Kipling), daughter of the recently deceased ruling monarch, Edward VII, forked out £3000 into the fund to set the ball rolling, while Rudyard did his bit by supporting the fund-raising effort, contributing some of his own booty and pressuring others to play the white man.

Since being pressured by Kipling was something akin to having one's fingernails extracted one by one, enough loot was raised quite quickly to build a small church. The foundation stone was laid in 1911 by no less a personage than Field Marshal Lord Roberts, the holy building work was completed in 1913 and the first liturgy took place in May 1914, about the time that Gavrilo Princip was busy assassinating the Archduke Ferdinand and the cosy Edwardian, now Georgian, world blew up. Such is the irony of history. It laughs scornfully at our feeble attempts to create certainty in an inherently unstable world and, like golf, slaps us in the face just when we think we have got everything sorted.

Because of the carnage taking place elsewhere in Europe, the brits left in their droves to make sure that they wouldn't miss out on their patriotic duty. St Georges began its long decline until it was rediscovered in 2005 by Donald Blevins. That story is now enshrined in these pages under the title of 'The Vicar's Tale. ' I recommend it. It makes interesting and poignant reading.

Vernet-les Bains Today

The present day Vernet is a pleasant place to live and to visit.

The luxurious villas constructed by its illustrious visitors are still in situ, though in need of some repair. The Casino still takes its income from those who haven't worked out, or don't care about, the odds of winning, and the Hotel du Portugal next door accommodates the great and the good at great and good prices. The Thermes still administer well-being and face-packs to the afflicted and massage the money from the well-heeled. The descendants of the swans in the park below still hiss at the children who come too close. The centre of the town is a pretty place to rest one's daily burden in the open air cafes and the view of the Canigou is resplendent. The sun still shines down for 300 days in the year radiating goodwill and bonhomie on the people. On the other 65 days there is nothing but gloom and despondency.

The monks still inhabit the monastery of St Martin and, for those with the masochistic urge to trek a mile up a very steep incline, it opens its doors to the weary traveller and the gawping grockel alike. Since it is a silent order there isn't much of a welcome patter, but the ambience of a thousand years of history lies all around.

In Michelin-speak Vernet is still worth a detour, especially for those whose bent lies in trudging the Pyrennean paths and breathing the clean pure air of the mountains. But please bring your warmest clothes in winter, and then some. This applies even in summer if you intend to ascend to the Chalet des Cortalets at 2000 metres in the jeep taxi, and then trudge to the top of Mount Canigou at 9000 feet. A simple zephyr below can be a raging tornado up there.

Up on the hill, in front of the church, the lone monument to the 1904 Entente has survived its 109 years of existence and receives the occasional spruce-up to assuage its loneliness. Its significance of course has long lost its edge, since the carve-up of Africa and the Middle East into French and English fiefdoms, which the entente was designed to set in stone, disappeared into the desire of countries to become masters of their own destiny. Which is an apt closing metaphor for today's Vernet les Bains.

And wouldn't you believe it but that ymmygrant wrote a poem about Vernet. That guy is really a glutton for punishment – or is it you - who have to read it?

Vernet les Bains – Paradise of the Pyrennees

Perched in its eyrie on Canigou's flank
Snuggling up close to Cady's right bank
Gateway to routes that lead to the peak
Vernet les Bains owns a pleasing mystique

Up on the mountain the water is clean
The air unpolluted and the setting serene
With wide open spaces, lined with high trees
Vernet, paradise of the high Pyrennees

Hot sulphured waters well up from the ground
The Therm's healing sources all the year round
No wonder that health is the township's main lure
Its special appeal is the art of the cure

Rheumatic ailments and poor respiration
All are well treated for improved purgation
Walking and cycling in the pure Vernet air
Assures well-being for the whole of the year.

Back in the last century's earlier days
The British invasion of Vernet held sway
Perfidious Albion at rest and at play
Taking the waters to eke out the day

Clerics and generals, the great and the good,
Victoria's daughter, and those of blue blood

Dukes and duchesses, and fat diplomats
The town overwhelmed by aristocrats.

This gathering of high-born came round the clock
To sample the wonders of la Belle Epoque
They came from all of Europe's rich nations
For gambling, the cure and just for vacations

Kipling the author came here with his wife
The waters would give her a much better life
A day at the therms calmed her articulations
While Kipling himself wrote his fine publications

To see Vernet best take the Kipling trail
That recounts his story in every detail
Start near the casino, a stylish delight
And follow it to every noteworthy site

The church of St George is worthy of heed
Built by subscription for the Anglican creed
Restored to its former glory last year
A cultural centre and a fit place for prayer

High on the top towering over the town
Is St Saturnin church, the jewel in its crown
A romaneque pesrl, rare relics and treasure
Proudly displayed for the visitor's pleasure

Across from the church a grand monument
Commemorates a momentous event
The Entente Cordiale whose colonial goal
To share states into French or British control

It's the only monument that portrays
This fine testament to imperial days
It owes its place in the town's history
To the good old British aristocracy

There's much more to see and do round Vernet
There's a wild life park in nearby Casteil

An eleventh century gem is next on the bill
Saint Martin du Canigou up on the hill

But, if you can, the thing that you must do
Is to reach the peak of the Canigou
A jeep will take you to where you can start
If you succeed you're a catalan at heart.

A place for reflection, a place to revere
A garden of Eden at all times of year
A place where good health permeates the air
Vernet les Bains waits to welcome you there

Norman Longworth

The little yellow train

Now you may think that the places I have already described would
be enough for a super sight-seeing holiday in the sun. I expect
that you have already been down to the travel agent to enquire‘
about how to get here. I'll deal with that later. But there is more –
much more. Take the little yellow train as a starting point from
Villefranche ststion. The little yellow train is such a feature of life
in this part of the Pyrennees – and, as a bonus, it is a fascinating
tale of death, determination, derring-do and deprivation.

The object of building the track was to connect the plain of the
Roussillon with the hanging valley of the Cerdagne some 35 kms
away and 2500 feet above, following the ever-narrowing course of
the river Têt. It is an audacious feat of engineering, the more so
because it was built in the first decade of the 20th century without
modern constructional aids, and entirely by the sweat and toil of
several thousands of manual workers. One has to make the
journey to realise just what an achievement that was. More than
20 bridges and viaducts, some of which span the whole valley, 45
miles of winding track and 15 remote stations serving the isolated
communities can be found on the way.

Over four years, men worked twelve hour days for a pittance and
many died in the building of it. In one particularly terrible incident
shortly before the line was open, the engineer in charge was
killed.

Disaster on the Track

His name, Ghisclard, is given to the spectacular suspension bridge three-quarters of the way up, which he designed and had built. On that fateful day it had been drizzling heavily and the train loaded with heavy rails made its way slowly to the steepest section of the track - a vertiginous, for a train, 1 in 30 slope. At this point, the records are not clear, but it is believed that some of the driver's mates forgot to insert the wedges which stopped the train from sliding backwards - it was twelve noon and at that time *déjeuner* calls to every Frenchman.

The crowded train began to slide backwards on the greasy rails, and the situation was not helped by the train controller announcing in loud panicky tones that the train was out of control. Soon the *'sauve qui peut'* message reached the brains of the passengers, some of whom promptly panicked and foolishly threw themselves out of the train and onto the rocks below. Perhaps they believed that flight was a better strategy than fight. Others, Ghisclard among them, took their chance on board and, as it left the rails, were carried over the edge of the parapet and crushed to death on impact.

So the chosen survival strategy didn't make much difference after all. Though many survived, Ghisclard the engineer was among the dead. A terrible rumpus ensued in the French Parliament. The Cerdagne deputy, Broussé, the driving force behind the construction of the railway, often in opposition to those who said it couldn't, or shouldn't, be done, was attacked as an assassin by other deputies in the parliament and work was suspended for several months.

The line was completed to the Cerdagne in 1910 but it was not until 16 years later that it reached its final destination, Latour de Carol on the border at the point where the trans-Pyrennean express from Toulouse to Barcelona enters Spain. There is a monument to engineer Ghisclard near to the point where he died by the bridge which bears his name, and another to Broussé, who made it all financially and logistically possible, in the centre of the roundabout at Mont Louis.

The little Yellow Train in Villefranche Station – journey on !

Riding the Train

The train trundles slowly and noisily out of Villefranche station and passes the Northern ramparts of the little town Vauban built. At this point for about 10 kilometres there is just room for a river, a road, a railway track and a few meadows, before the mountain sides sheer out of the valley at each side. After Serdanya and Joncet, two pretty villages hugging the valley bottom in an indiscriminate huddle of haphazard but delightful cottages, the mountains begin to close in and the over imaginative and the claustrophobic experience their first incipient sensation of approaching panic.

To the left there is nothing but damp, vertical rock just feet from the window. To the right one can look downwards over sheer cliffs into the river valley some 90 feet below. The train now desperately hugs the mountain side as it crawls and sways up the mountain track, towards the village of Olette. The higher it climbs the deeper grows the ravine on the right until the vertigo sufferers refuse to approach the windows and sit, eyes closed and shaking, in the middle seats. Those in the open-top carriages get the full treatment.

Then as the train passes the old mineral extraction plant, still working until 1994 – producing bauxite, tin, silver, zinc and a variety of other precious metals - the valley opens out slightly and the passengers emerge, blinking in the unaccustomed sunlight, into Olette station. Olette is an animated little village marking the western extreme of the Conflent. It's main purpose in life appears to be as an involuntary collection point for traffic from both directions.

Because the valley is quite narrow at this point and the road through the town was not built for modern traffic technology or conditions, there isn't overmuch parking space for the cars of the villagers and their visitors. And so the obstinate Olettian who wishes to make a point will park his car on the narrow main street while a queue of angry cars gathers behind an oil tanker which can't quite squeeze past it and has therefore stopped the traffic in both directions. It is also the only village between Prades and the Cerdagne with a petrol station and this contributes even less to the alleviation of the traffic problem.

After Olette the valley tapers inwards and the railway track clings even closer to the south side of the mountain. Past narrow defiles and through sullen tunnels it rises, above the prettily-coloured sanatorium of *Thuès les Bains* where asthmatics congregate and heavy breathing is the norm, crossing the entrance to the *Gorges de Carança*, one of the great walks of the area, and on to the *Pont Séjourne*.

Here it has to cross the valley to achieve the semblance of a trackhold and all the best photographs of the train are taken as it seems to balance, Houdini-like, on the bridge way above the valley floor like a yellow-costumed centipede on a tight-rope. From the train, cars pass like ant-trails beneath the arches and those suffering from vertigo withdraw even further into their own personal and psychological huddle.

The village of *Fontpédrouse* seems to pass laboriously by and, beyond it, the tiny outline of the baths at *St Thomas les Bains* makes a fleeting appearance in a cleft of the valley opposite. This is strange and wonderful place, well-known to the many people who come from far and wide to clean out the pores once a week. Two enormous open-air Jacuzzis cool the naturally-scalding water from the inner mountain down to just below blood temperature, and human beings wallow there like contented hippopotami. The best time is in the middle of winter when the outside temperature is below zero and the frost is on the ground. Skiers call in on their descent of the valley to join the wallowing, and to ease the aches and pains of a day unsuccessfully attempting to remain vertical.

The train now really begins to struggle. The gradient here is so severe that one can understand how that catastrophe more than 100 years ago came to happen at this point. Here too the road winds up hairpin after hairpin crossing the railway line at one of its steepest points. Those in the train look out across the valley onto blue-black mountain crags, sombre in the shadow of the morning sun, and down into the gorge below. It seems to sink forever into a twilight sunless never-never world where trolls guard the entrance to their caves and where witches stir the broth in their cauldrons, only making guest appearances on the hilltop each Walpurgisnacht.

Across Ghisclaine's suspension bridge and past the monument to his genius, the valley suddenly opens out and there is a sunlit journey along gentle slopes until the train breasts the rise into the Cerdagne and comes to a gentle halt at the station of Mont Louis. This tribute to Vauban's military talents is a top-of-the-valley mirror of Villefranche at the bottom. Its bastion-broad walls protected the village within from marauding Spaniards and discourage their descent into the lower depths to plunder and pillage. Not that, if they had any sense, they would want to do that, but this is the 20th and not 17th century and who can understand such bellicose motivations some 300 years later?

Another ten miles and the train pulls in at Odeilla, the station below the town of Font Romeu where the majority of passengers disembark, stretch their limbs and re-adjust their travel-weary minds. A bus takes them to this bustling tourist *station de ski et de montagne*, and past the solar furnace which testifies that this is one of the sunniest areas of Europe by putting several thousand kilowatts of sun-generated energy into the French national grid every day. A museum explaining its *modus operandum* and *raison d'être* is visitable at its base.

Meanwhile the train proceeds for a further 30 miles, slowly winding its way across the domesticated slopes of the Cerdagne towards its final destiny with the trans-Pyrennean express at Latour de Carol.

More?

Who could want for more, but wait, of course there IS more within easy reach of the Conflent. Forty minutes away are the shores of the blue Mediterranean , pretty seaside resorts such as Argeles sur mer, Canet and St Cyprien, picturesque fishing ports like Port Vendres and Collioure, seawater museums at Banyuls sur mer, former home of Jacques Cousteau , and, for those with fewer inhibitions, the naturist beaches of Leucate.

The picture postcard port of Collioure

In the mountains, again 40 minutes away, there are the skiing resorts of Les Angles, Pyrenees 2000 and Font Romeu where, in winter, people mess about on plastic planks and the French winter sports teams have been known to practise. There are hiking pistes for every taste and level, riding schools, painting classes, car expeditions both scenically gentle and jaw-droppingly vertiginous, and natural beauty in every direction. Here is paradise.

Getting here

So now that you have been convinced –and how could you not be - I will tell you how to get here. Though the Conflent is a hidden paradise, getting to it is not difficult. For the discerning traveller who prefers to maximise his chances of remaining alive, and to avoid the potential carnage of the French motorways, it is, perhaps surprisingly, still accessible by train from everywhere in Europe. A local branch line traces its way from village to village up the Têt valley from Perpignan. Through communities with, for us, evocative names it meanders - Millas where the bulls run through the village at the July Feria time; Ille-sur-Têt, a celebrated centre of sacred baroque art; Vinça, with its beach by the lake and its beautiful old centre, to Prades and Villefranche, where it connects with the little yellow train .

And soon, the almighty TGV is coming - to Perpignan of course, not to Prades. The new line from Avignon to Montpellier is already in an advanced state of construction despite frequent austerity drives. The route of its extension through Béziers and Narbonne to Perpignan has now been laboriously negotiated, and the right brown paper envelopes passed on to the right people. Within 4 years we should see the TGV speeding like a jet-fuelled diplodocus from Montpellier to Perpignan – ever closer to paradise.

Here and there are signs that this is a serious business in several parts of the *département*. The new Perpignan international station, has been erected complete with Salvador Dali's *'Centre du Monde'* label, and one can even now ride with the TGV beneath the Pyrennean massif to the fleshpots of Barcelona. Fast rockets will complete the journey from Paris in four and a half hours, from Calais in five and a half, and from other parts of continental Europe in half the time it presently takes. Barcelona is a mere hour away from Perpignan instead of the ambling three and a half hours it used to waste.

For those who need their own personal transport system but would not wish to risk the drive of hundreds of miles, the autorail is an alternative way of taking the strain. Calais or Boulogne to Narbonne overnight can be a restful experience and leave just one hour of nervous driving to reach the Conflent. It is infinitely quicker and more efficient than it used to be, though not, unfortunately, any less expensive. Beware though of the Catalan drivers when you arrive. Japanese kami-kazi pilots had more regard for life. If you don't believe me, read the driver's tale in volume 3.

If sustainability isn't your bag and you really want to increase your carbon footprint, your last alternative is by air. Every Saturday evening, car-loads of British Conflent-dwellers descend the 45 kilometres from Prades to Perpignan Airport to muster their loved ones from the Ryanair and Flybe flights which ply the route from Stansted, Birmingham and Dublin each week in the summer. Two weeks later, physically and mentally exhausted, nerves raw and visible at the ends of their fingers, faces haggard and tense, most of them make the same journey in reverse to re-deposit them gratefully on the plane home and, in the case of those who haven't yet worked out that one needs at least a week's rest between visiting hordes, to collect up the next contingent.

Some of the more adventurous Brits will make a longer two hour trek to Montpellier, Girona, Carcassonne and Beziers, where daily aeroplanes fly from and to London, Manchester, Edinburgh and other destinations. Those unlucky enough to have visitors flying to Barcelona have verily drawn the short straw. A voyage which on kilometrage should take just over two hours, actually takes three because the signposts to the airport seem to be inexplicably missing at crucial places and they inevitably lose themselves in the mysteries of the big city on the way there.

Having arrived at their destination and accomplished their obligatory tryst, they will make the return journey and follow the roads marked France. Should they do so they will find themselves heading for Tarragona to the South and spend an equally frustrating hour or two retracing their steps. The Road to Barcelona is a journey most people will avoid at all costs, but the TGV will change all of that. In future visitors can reach Perpignan in a trice and be whisked off from there to all parts of the region.

So now you know. Paradise is but a short journey away from where you now are. *Venez nombreux* as they say in these parts – come in large numbers and be sure that, if you do, you will receive a warm Catalan welcome. So come up and see me sometime.

See you here in Paradise.

Naomi

Tales of the Conflent

Chapter the Syxth

The Choyr-Leaders Tale
or
Makyng Musyk yn the Conflent

**Being the tale of how harmonious intentions
became transformed into musical madness**

The Choir Leaders tale

The upper church in our village is, by common consent, a marvel of acoustics. Even the village choir sounds good in it, though since it is a true village choir open to all without audition, not all of the sounds are the most harmonious ever heard to the glory of God. To introduce myself properly, my name is Valerie and I'm privileged to be the leader of the famous Eus chorale – famous anyway in the village of Eus. Before moving to this demi-Paradise

I took my musical training in the posh conservatoires of the Northern climes. Donizetti, Mozart, Verdi, Rossini – all grist to my musical mill and a voice that most of my choir say has a certain nightingalian quality. I would not of course make any such claim, but it's interesting to be compared to a night-bird. Deposited here in the peculiar musical traditions of the Conflent, it all seems to be a million kilometres from there.

I didn't of course come here specifically to run the local choir. Perhaps I had in mind something more challenging – Covent Garden or the Sydney Opera House, or even La Scala. However it proved rather difficult to get to rehearsal from here and they were exceedingly reluctant to come to the Conflent for their musical training, paradise or not. So, one day when I wasn't thinking carefully enough, I received a telephone call from a cousin of a cousin inviting, indeed challenging, me to help continue the great philharmonic traditions of Eus village, and here I am. And it's certainly challenging!

But I have learned. How I have learned! Lesson number one is that running a village choir is a little like searching for the philosopher's stone – we try to produce golden notes out of distinctly base musical metal. As I remember it, not even the greatest alchemists in Europe ever found the secret. But they had a great time trying, and I'm also having a trying time. Having said that, I love it, I love my Cant'Eus and I love to make music however dissonant, as do we all in my choir. Practice night is often a case of never mind the notes, feel the music.

Close proximity to tonality becomes one more triumph, as does one less groan from those whose only familiarity with pitch is at the USAP Rugby ground. But to be a little more respectful to my hard-working singers, the quality is not as low as all that. We sing in competitions and at the local *rassemblements* with and against other choirs and we are far from the worst. Which of course is saying very little!

The choir is finely and evenly balanced between sopranos, altos, tenors and basses and in each there is an equally even mix of those who hit the note, those who think they have hit it and haven't, and those who send out a search party for it with little idea of where, or how, to find it. Tone-deafness is an occupational hazard for an equal number of people in each section. Some members are there more because it's hugely preferable to watching French TV (vomiting in the toilet would be preferable to that), and perhaps, too, for the free wine at the end of the proceedings (and on the many other occasions when a sense of thirst must be slaked.)

In spite of this, some songs we get completely right, more by good luck, I suspect, than any particular magic on my part. Others we get almost right and there are a goodly number of tunes around which we are continually fighting a rearguard action, if not activating an undisciplined rout. Sometimes we think we have got it surrounded but somehow it escapes to fight again another day.

We even have some star performers. My choir is enhanced by its international brigade, the second in Catalonia within the last 70 years, but this time an invasion with peaceful intent. Nine English, two Welsh, five Dutch, several from Catalonia du Sud, (a part of Spain, though never say that openly to a real Catalan!), and six

Parisians (down here regarded as another country, full of enemies of the people) make music with about forty local people from Eus and the villages around. We sing to whoever is rash enough to ask us and wherever we are invited; we sing at festivals; we sing at weddings and funerals, we invite other choirs and sing with them. And if, through bitter experience, no-one asks us to sing to them, we sing to ourselves for the sheer joy of singing, between courses at the frequent village feasts, in the streets as we leave the Thursday *répétition*, and at parties which can happen as often as four times a week. No occasion is safe but that it cannot be celebrated by a loud, vaguely musical, racket.

Many Eus choral occasions rest in my memory but one magic day in the Cerdagne is particularly powerful. It was a celebration of singing by six choirs from both sides of the border and took place in the courtyard of the *Hermitage*, a 13th century monastery, now turned into a restaurant - perhaps a poignant but true comment on our times. The last item of the concert was a rendering of the Catalonian National Anthem *'El Segadors'* by the combined power of all the choirs. It is a rousing anthem, all the more so for being a bloodthirsty description of the use of scythes by thousands of catalan peasants in battle, and the somewhat divisive effect this can have on the anatomical structure of attacking forces. This being Catalonia, the said bodies would normally be the hated Castilians. The foreigners at least have the excuse that they don't understand most of the words of the anthem, which goes into considerable physiological detail. But its simple harmonies sung at full blast by more than 300 fervent chorists produced, I am sure, a frisson factor of considerable magnitude for the audience. For my choir it was quite simply *formidable*.

Répétition, or practice, day is Tuesday. The unwary visitor can, completely *gratuit* and for nothing, listen to us in full practice warble at the Eus village hall. It is scheduled to start at 5,30 pm but, this being France, it rarely gets into vocal motion before 6. Firstly, everyone has to run the full gauntlet of the French welcoming culture and, among more than 40 people, the lip-cheek contact hours mount dramatically. The actual mathematical expression is, I believe, 40 Shriek! 40+39+38+37....etc, and that's also a good word to use in the context of my sopranos. This process takes up an inordinate amount of time. The hall is awash with the peculiar 'pchou' sounds of people expressing their osculatory greetings. Most of the women make it easy by proferring the cheek to be lightly touched, and will even provide the necessary sound effects, but some do not show as much enthusiasm as others. Perhaps they are sensitive to the reluctance of our more northerly members, coming from colder climes and therefore by definition with colder hearts, to embrace the custom.

The second barrier to a timely start is the apparent inability of the members to be silent for more than a split-second. They are a cheerful crowd, bringing to each new meeting the obligation to unburden themselves of everything that has happened since the last one, and it is a pleasure to be in the midst of such contented chatter. However, once the beloved great leader, as I am known by a discerning few, has at last established some semblance of her authority on the proceedings, we commence by vocalising. And how my choir vocalises! Up the scales and down the arpeggios they soar, across the crotchets and quavers they glide, some more in tune and in time than others, until it is time to burst victoriously into the choral repertoire. But here there is another small lacuna.

My choir sings mostly in Catalan and French and for the former (and often for the latter, bearing in mind its composition) there lies in wait the small problem of pronouncing the words correctly. The nuances of the Catalan language mean that most v's are b's, many, but not all. E's are a's depending on where they occur in the word, and some o's are oo's. Those choir members of Catalan origin act as strict minders on these occasions, pouncing hard upon each mispronunciation as if it were a capital offence, and turning our thoughts and mouths toward the straight and narrow of linguistic purity. But the real point of the exercise is to enjoy melody-making, and that is an objective fully and heartily achieved. *Répétition* night is a landmark of the week and hugely enjoyed. It is followed by a small snack of nibbles, bottles of *ricard* and the local *vin doux* and yet more animated chatter until the small hours.

Each Easter Monday, the Chorale performs the charming 'Goigs del Ous', the catalonian name for the festival of the eggs which

seems to occur up in so many cultures at Easter time. This entails
dressing the women in the gaily coloured Catalan costume of
white blouses, bright red full skirts and black shawls

The men for their part are even more flamboyant in their full
rooster splendour of *barotine*, phage, and a white shirt held
together by a sort of string tie in the Catalan *'sang et or'* colours.
The *barotine* might best be described as a bright red off-centre
pixie hat whose peak hangs over the forehead like that of a
rampant cock.

The spring-time symbolism of this is of course no accident. The phage is also bright red and wraps around the midriff in the manner of a cummerbund. More of it goes round some than others, and since many of the choir are chronologically, as well as dimensionally, challenged, a disproportionate ratio of white hair adds a further touch of colourful contrast.

Thus dazzlingly regaled off we go, ageing rampant cocks and psychedelic women, to beg harmoniously in the streets of the village for our Easter nourishment. As we sing suggestive songs about food, we lay out in front of us the '*cistellas*', baskets into which we hope the grateful inhabitants of the village will place their offerings of *ous* (eggs), *botifarra* (sausages), *pa* (bread) and of course wine, the more the better.

To maximise our opportunities we sing in all 5 of the pretty little '*places*' hidden in the recesses of this wonderful village, and even often spend the previous evening singing at the outlying farms. No-one therefore escapes their responsibility to make the choir fatter and jollier, unless they remember that urgent visit to Aunt Sophie on the other side of the mountain in time.

And, bless them, they do contribute. After all, this is tradition and the local people are strongly in favour of that. This year we collected 450 eggs, 120 bottles of wine, 50 baguettes and innumerable sausages and other nourritures, enough to feed a small multitude. We tend to leave the idea of loaves and fishes to Higher Authorities, more competent to optimise their possibilities.

Having completed our melodic task we then repair, groupies trailing, to the *maison du temps libre* to make an inventory of our booty, and to fabricate an enormous omelette, laced with mushrooms, sausages, herbs and a number of secret ingredients best left unmentioned, and, of course, to drink the wine.

When we are replete, we sing and we dance and we celebrate the joy of being alive amidst such beauty and bonhomie.

But the zenith of chorale activity takes place every other year in the '*spectacle*' a sort of end of the pier show with choral music. It entails a rich and heady mixture of music and acting and gives those Depardieu manqués the opportunity to demonstrate their thespian skills, such as they are. Last year my singers, as I loosely call them for want of a more accurate description, decided to write their own script based on the history of the village through the ages. The inspiration behind this was the former village schoolma'am, a lively and garrulous lady with a finely tuned sense of humour usually based on toilet matters and raunchy gender relationships.

And I have to say that she did a fine job. The village's technicolourful past was laid bare for all to see, though I suspect that the interpretation of some events owed more to the application of a creative mind than to researched historical fact. Anyway, be that as it may, it certainly provided a challenge and one enthusiastically accepted, as you will see.

The whole piece started with the Adam and Eve story. It is not generally known that the Garden of Eden had the site of our village at its centre – some place it a few thousand miles away – but there for all to see was the real truth. '*The first man on the earth*' burbled the choir in Catalan '*was called Adam, a Catalan,*' while Marianne, a pendulously proportioned Dutch lady acted out the temptation of Eve with an equally generously proportioned Frenchman. One can understand that the wardrobe department was not overstretched in this part of the show, though certain standards of 21st century decorum had to be applied. While French villages are not noted for their reticence in matters sexual, it all tends to take place behind closed doors.

And indeed it was a tour de force. It is generally understood that Adam, egged on by the serpent, seduced Eve in the Garden. Marianne was having none of that. Being Dutch, role reversal came easily to her. She threw herself into the task of tempting Adam with determined gusto and not a little seductive skill. Indeed poor Adam, and the audience and the choir, were subjected to the whole gamut of feminine invention in this department. The eyes of the young farmers in the stalls closest to the action stood out on stalks. This was experiential education in the raw. At one point the blanket covering their modesty moved as if she was about to try to single-handedly generate the population of the world as quickly as feasible, as well as reverse the local reputation of Dutch females in the vicinity (in this region the Dutch are well known for their dykes in both the ancient and modern sense of the word).

Meanwhile Adam, who had been subjected to this relentless barrage of womanly affection, grew redder and redder. This was not a role for the faint-hearted – indeed for anyone with a suspect ticker – and I feared for his life at times. After all the average age of the chorale is more than a little over 60 and it was having great difficulty concentrating on the words. '*Adam tasted milk and honey from the land*' they sang in slightly strangled voices, '*He let temptation lead him on*', while Marianne did her best to oblige.

But it all went off well without our having to summon the ambulance, and the future of humanity in the world, or at least in this small corner of it, was assured. As Marianne left the stage, the whole audience, which had been studying her technique with interest, cheered her efforts to the roof.

The next piece celebrated the 'Homme de Tautavel', a 450,000 year old stone age man found in good condition in one of the nearby villages. Since his discovery in 1920, he has spawned a whole industry in the region. If only he could have known at the time how he would have been exploited, he might not have taken the precaution of burying himself in peat. Be that as it may, the portrayal was little short of a masterpiece. The renaissanced homme was Jean-Paul, the churchwarden. He has also cropped up in the Mayor's tale (volume 2), sadistically collecting unsuspecting tourists in the village church. Perfect for the part, and dressed convincingly in a simian costume, he set about recreating 'planet of the apes' in his own image.

'Homme de tau, homme de ta, homme de vel', trilled the choir in perfect unison, *'Apparut d'une etre bizarre proche parent d'l'orang-utang.'* Upon which, Jean-Paul leapt into the audience wielding his plastic cudgel to beat the bejasus out of any one who had crossed him during the previous 40 years. We could all tell that this was real aggression therapy at work. While the choir sang about how the original had dealt summarily with woolly mammoths, sabre-toothed tigers, mountain lions and such, Jean-Paul dispensed vengeance equally summarily upon his human enemies, real and imagined. Anyone who might have entertained a bad thought about him came in for the treatment.

The milk of human kindness normally expected of a man of the church was singularly lacking. There was no mercy and no forgiveness. The onslaught lasted perhaps for 3 minutes, the time it took to sing the song, and it was only with a loud roll on the piano that I was able to snap him out of his ferocious mind-set and get him to reluctantly leave the floor, a man wholly-satisfied and purged of his demons. Much more successful and much more exciting than the psychiatrist's couch or the cave-painting therapy we sang about, though the expressions on some of the sore heads in the audience did not give the impression that this was the end of the matter for them. He did however receive some sympathetic applause from those who had escaped the blitz.

We wound rapidly forward into the time of the Greeks, who had landed some years BC on the coast and made forays inland from time to time. And now the village was portrayed as the centre of one bacchanalian orgy after another. It must have been an interesting time, if one had the stamina. We managed to find 5 basses who could sing the well-known medieval drinking song '*Tourdion*' approximately in tune – the subject matter helped. And as they sang, comely mythological (in every sense) wenches and vestal virgins (even more mythological) gyrated sinuously around them, enticing them with lotus to eat and carafes of wine to drink. Bacchus himself would have been proud of their performance. For all of them it rolled back the years when, as comely maidens themselves, they cavorted meaningfully around prospective husbands and enticed them into the arms of Aphrodite (this is after all a work of fiction).

The basses were unfazed. They resisted manfully every blandishment thrown in their way, though we had to impose a 'no touching' policy on the proceedings after a disastrous practice session, and it also helped that every one of them was well over 60 years old. *'Let's drink well'*, they chanted *'Drink my friends drink and sing gaily, By drinking a hogshead, Bacchus will reward us and we'll have a party.'* The words might be banal in English, but in French they take on a whole new, and more hopeful, meaning, especially when surrounded by frolicking maid-servants with designs upon influencing their immediate future.

Anyway, the audience, which by this time had made up its collective mind to enjoy itself come what may, cheered the brave basses off the stage. By the look in the eyes of some of the unaccompanied males standing behind the free seats at the back of the hall, they would not necessarily have exhibited the same impressive restraint, vestal virgins or not.

Time passes. The village manages to sleep uneasily through the dark ages and through successive invasions by the barbarian hordes including the famous Goth family – Ostro, Visi and the just plain Goths – and, just for light relief, the Vandals. *Plus ca change*…. It is all too reminiscent of their present day equivalents, the English, the Dutch, the Swedes. All in all life became pretty miserable, with a shortage of everything that made life worth living – bread, fuel, Kellogg's corn flakes, pedigree cat food, tenors who can sing in tune, the lottery, radio 4….

All of this was portrayed beautifully by the choir and its amateur Oliviers. *'La Part a Dieu'* a plaintive (how well we do plaintive!) lament requesting alms, did its best to stir the souls of the audience to their deepest limits. The melody starts ultra-pianissimo, almost silently, becomes raise-the-roof fortissimo in the middle and then fades away into silence at the end. I have to admit that the audience seemed to appreciate the beginning and the end best of all.

But it's what was happening on the floor of the house that matters. One village's misfortune in times past is the same village's opportunity today. And didn't they take it well. Bands of

uncouth, unkempt, unsavoury and frankly menacing choristic
characters dressed as beggars roamed around the corridors of
the hall holding out caps, plastic bags, dustbin lids – anything
that would hold large amounts of money. Anyone in the audience
showing a reluctance to contribute to the performance was
threatened with a re-run of the homme de tautavel, this time with a
real cudgel. Few defied such an ordonnance, but there were
pockets of resistance in the middle of the rows where people
pretended to pay the protection money and actually didn't.

So while this approach was moderately successful, it was Joos's
performance that took the biscuit. Joos, you will remember, is the
tennis-playing, cadaverous Dutch resident whose daughter found
herself a French husband here many years ago. God knows what
Joos did for a living in Holland, but here he transformed himself
into the most pitiable human being on earth. The beggars in the
Paris metro are well-to-do toffs in contrast to him. Around his
head was wrapped an old towel that looked like it had been buried
in the neighbour's byre for 200 years. His ragged trousers would
not have been amiss on Methusaleh. His shirt seemed to have
been a recent feast for rats. His shoes were miserably soleless.

As he shuffled and limped around the hall like a distressed zombie on a pair of crutches fashioned from branches of the tree outside his house, people nearest to the aisles visibly cringed and moved away for fear of what he might give them. In return, he made it silently obvious that what he did or did not give to them very much depended on what *they* gave to him. Subtle it wasn't, effective it was. Hardened farmers, accustomed to losing crops, animals and womenfolk to the vagaries of weather and oppression, wept inconsolably as he passed by, while their womenfolk dug deep into the nether regions of their handbags in en effort to put the unfortunate mendicant out of his misery.

And all the while the mournful notes of 'La part a Dieu' rang out from the front of the hall. '*We have no bread to feed our babes, If you have bread give it to us*' and '*We have no–one to sleep with at night, if you have daughters make them available.*' This last entreaty met with precious little sympathy. Very few would have let their daughters within a mile of Joos, but if the lesser evil involved being a few coins poorer, then so be it. At the end of the song, a pregnant silence reigned. The audience had arrived in large numbers for a free show, and it was trying to work out just how it had been relieved of far more than it would have paid as an entrance fee. The stillness was broken only by the chink of money from behind the choir as the beggars counted their ill-gotten gains.

Things took a turn for the better in the village at the turn of the first millennium. The dark ages were over and the middle ages began. Passing quietly over a certain invasion of the Northern lands by Bill the Conqueror (it would have taken two centuries for the news to get through to Eus, and even then it might not have made it past the decision-makers in the mediaeval newsroom as worthy of broadcast), we reached the time of the troubadours, wandering bands of minstrels who came to enliven the cheerless lot of the toilers of the soil in every village, including ours. It seems that the whole of the south of France was heaving with colourfully-apparelled love-sick Lotharios singing their hearts out to mandolin accompaniment before the window of their chosen loved ones or the day. Bands of joyful gypsies roamed on permanent tour complete with roadies and instruments. It has its equivalent today as the aging Stones, the even more aging three tenors, the positively ancient Johnny Halliday and his group and a panoply of electric guitarists, manic drummers and strangled singers tour from city to city in search of youthful adulation.

But musical it definitely was, and so my choir rose to commemorate the arrival of the baladins with a song called appropriately *'les Baladins'*. As it mangled the notes with an enthusiasm born of short practise times – we could have used another two years for that – a group of erstwhile sopranos and tenors exercised their terpsichorial skills in the hall, while an amateur accordionist – the ymmygrant I believe - dug out his hundred year old out of tune instrument from the dust of the garage and circulated the hall. Those he passed somehow found reason to stick their fingers in their ears, pretending to have found an itinerant piece of wax in there. The Mayor of the village became Harlequin, dancing through the audience and phrenetically worrying his tambourine as if in search of another mandate in the village hot seat. The local doctor came up with a fetching little number in multicoloured stripes and eagerly banged his maraccas as if summoning nurses to the operating theatre.

But the stars of the show were the ladies. Never before has so much bare matronly midriff jellied and bobbled in a cold climate, as they pirouetted and pranced their way along the corridors of the hall. The farmers' eyes opened wide at this vast expanse of flesh never before seen in public, and often not even in private, while their wives feared for their future. Even those farmers whose wives were among the dancers discovered new territory. This being February not so much goose as donkey bumps ruled. It was difficult to tell them from the real thing.

By now the audience didn't care. The Eus *Folies Bergères* was in full flow. '*Les baladins qui serpentent les routes*' burbled out the choir in a passable imitation of togetherness, '*Viennent de loin parmi les champs de ble*'. But no-one was listening to the words, uplifting though they were, as the elderly matrons, temporarily liberated from all inhibition, lost themselves in a frenzy of the dancing arts, spinning and whirling with gay abandon.

Although I had my work cut out keeping the chorale to something approximating to the tune, I'll swear that I caught one of them out of the corner of my eye, having been to ballet lessons some 40 years before, trying to recreate the pliés and the pas de deux of the yesteryear she had almost forgotten. She seemed to finish with a splits which could be heard in the next village. Whatever, she didn't turn up at the next choir practise, and seemed to walk with a careful and peculiar gait for weeks afterwards. The piece ended to great applause from the men and a restrained pursed-lips silence from the women in the audience. Perhaps if the Mayor had peeled off a little more, it would have been different.

The era of Louis XIV, the Sun King and chief author of the hexagon that is modern-day France, was fairly important to our village. Previously we had been reigned over by a succession of feudal chiefs, the Kings of Aragon, the Dukes of Majorca and an assortment of worthies belonging to what we now call Spain. All of a sudden we became French with the signing of the treaty of the Pyrennees in 1659. Not that it affected life in the village overmuch. It was still a tough life, always on the edge of starvation for most villagers. They had the added excitement of occasional bloody Tet valley offensives by the Spanish army, who were not exactly gruntled at losing their territory so easily. In one of these raids the whole village was put to the fire. No lives were lost since the inhabitants had shrewdly retired to the countryside, but the event didn't exactly increase the per capita wealth of a region that wasn't rolling in prosperity before. So dear young Louis felt that he had to make a visit to the far-flung parts of his new empire to reassure his new subjects, and Eus was allegedly included in the itinerary.

Well, of course we have a song for all occasions and this was no exception. We dug up '*La Polka du Roi*' a seventeenth century *minuet risqué* with a storyline that would make a maiden blush if this were not France, where blushing maidens are in very short supply. But then, in this country there is not so much a cavalier attitude to lewdness as a specific requirement that it should be made law. It took four verses to tell of the marquis' ultimately successful attempt to dance himself into the marquise's bloomers (the successful culmination was not included in the show), largely because the said garment was deeply buried under several layers of fabric.

'*ah-ah-ah-ah, Entrons en danse, quelle cadence,ah-ah-ah-ah*' sang the chorale, '*c'est la Polka du Roi*', while four of its more elegant members danced the stately minuet in the full costume of the time. This in itself was a triumph of will over circumstance since, although the month was cold, the inside of the hall had become so hot, presumably because of the previous piece, that the four were perspiring even before they reached the stage. It did not make for a successful event. The dance requires a complicated exchange of partners in strict sequence, but so befuddled were the dancers by the heat, the unaccustomed length of the womens' dresses, the extreme tightness of the mens' trousers causing involuntary twitches, and the inability of anyone in my choir to adhere to simple rules, that it turned out to be something of a disaster.

'*Moi pour l'amour je suis toujours pret*' goes the third verse, and it is here that the inevitable happened. A single couple that should have crossed in the middle found itself competing for the same territory with the other couple, which had jumped the sequential gun. Attempts to remedy the situation quickly resulted in one of the men trampling on the Marquise's dress, such that she was unable to move in any direction except downwards, which she promptly did.

The audience cheered loudly believing, or perhaps hoping, that this was part of the plot. And of course it was in perfect keeping with the progress of the song in which, by this time, the marquis had considerably advanced his primary objective and was busily preparing for the denouement.

'J'enleve votre jolie robe, et doucement j'ouvre votre corset, votre perruque est mal commode, il faut vous en debarrasser,' trilled the tenor at the side of the group, himself longing to enter into the spirit of the piece. However, before events could progress beyond the acceptable (even in France), the accompanying couple decided to do something about the chaos on the floor of the stage and tried to help a reluctant Marquis and a flustered Marquise to

their feet. At which point the song ran out of verses and the four beat a hasty retreat to the dressing room, the wild applause of the crowd ringing loudly in their ears. It is not recorded what happened there, but there were more than several minutes of delay before they returned to the choir.

The next century saw the revolution and of course there is no way that a red-blooded Frenchman can be prevented from celebrating the gruesome massacres that took place at that time. In our repertoire, we had any number of melodic possibilities from the Marseillaise downwards to choose from, but eventually we sang *'La Carmagnole'*, depicting the *'sans culottes',* a group of gullible, and if French history is to be believed, lovable knickerless female thugs who spread anarchy around Paris in the late 18th century, while others, such as Robespierre, were trying to bring order by decapitating everyone in possession of a *perruquet*. This was followed by a marching song called *'Le Depart'* which describes how eagerly revolutionary soldiers followed a certain Monsieur Napoleon into battle for the glory of *la patrie.*

This was not the highlight of creativity in the *spectacle*. The *Carmagnoles* comprised a group of six aged choir members (who might indeed have been the sons and daughters of the originals) skipping and frolicking around the hall like two-year olds and carrying an elongated red, white and blue standard of France, much to the mystification of the audience who didn't quite know what it was all about. The chorale did its best to inform them through the six verses.

'Antoinette decided to send us flying onto our bums' they warbled in French in indistinct voice, *'and Louis had promised to be faithful to his country, so let's dance the Carmagnole to celebrate their demise,'* as the tempo of the chase increased in direct proportion to the murder count. But the result of all this effort, as the puffing and breathless pseudo-carmagnoles crawled to the front completely knackered after the fourth tour of the hall, was a continuing puzzlement in the body of the hall about their sanity. It got a cheer though – after all the beloved flag was involved for whatever unfathomable reason. And the choir had finished singing.

For '*Le Depart*' the casting Director must have been drunk. Four out of the five worthies stamping at the front of the stage in patriotic tune to the birth of the glorious republic, and death to all its enemies, turned out to be local Brits. Perhaps they didn't initially understand the words, but they were simple enough, and as it dawned upon them what they were marching to, the stamping grew more and more self-conscious and less and less enthusiastic and convincing. Glances were thrown at each other, as the choir chanted '*The war trumpets have sounded, death to the enemies of France, let the blood be spilled.*' After all, the main said enemy was actually at the front of the stage stamping away with progressively less enthusiasm in front of an excited crowd of potential patriotic warriors.

Meanwhile the lone Frenchman, who also had his own drum to beat, continued to give a credible imitation of a man ready to die immediately for his *patrie*.

Indeed he might well have done so, since there were another six verses, and beating ones feet incessantly on the floor for five whole minutes while carrying a heavy drum certainly takes it out on a man. Luckily, no-one in the audience became inflamed with too much patriotic fervour, and anyway it was the weekend. So, exhausted, he faded quietly into the ranks of the chorale to wonder at his misplaced endeavour, while the Brits, suitably chagrined by the experience, also slunk shame-facedly away. Nevertheless, such was the passion generated by the sight of grown men celebrating a time when France actually won a battle, that the audience gave them all a big hand for their efforts. Thus was the glorious revolution re-created in the 21st century in our village.

It's at this point that I get to sing all by myself. Well a little quality doesn't come amiss amid all the previous strangulations. The full three verses and choruses of 'Les trois cloches' are my *'specialité de la maison',* much as I understand *'les compagnons de la chanson'* rendered the song an unmissable event on *'Family Favourites'* in Britain during the 1940s (some of my choir members can actually remember it!). It was popular here in France too, and we even sang it in the right language.

It's about the lifespan of a typically French villager before the age of mass travel. He comes into the world, is baptised in the church, gets hitched in the same church, has children and eventually goes the way of all of us, and is buried in the churchyard. Deep but simple philosophical musings that strike a resonance with many of the villagers hereabouts. The chorale is expected to hum lightly and meaningfully in the background while I do my stuff. However hum is not quite the right word for this strange sound – more the unsteady drone of an aeroplane with serious engine trouble. Survivors of the London blitz and the doodlebugs would know it well. Indeed, some of the older British onlookers kept casting anxious glances through the hall window.

Well, I know how to milk an audience, so that, despite the aeromodeller's practice session in the background, I gave Jean Nicot's birth, marriage and death the full no-holds-barred tear-jerking works. When I had finished there wasn't a dry eye in the house. And a silence while everyone in the house contemplated his own impending mortality. I swear that I saw a couple of older members sneak outside to ring the funeral parlour. But then the subsequent applause threatened to bring the house down, literally, making it difficult to continue the show.

But continue it did. For some, no doubt scandalous, reason, a discreet veil seemed to be drawn over the village's 19th century. As the Ramsbottom family were wont to say about Blackpool beach, 'Nobody killed and nobody drownded – in fact nowt to laugh at at all.' It is as if the restoration of the monarchy, the July plot, Louis Napoleon, the Crimean hostilities, the 1848 second revolution, the franco-prussian conflict and the Paris commune had not existed. And of course, as far as this village in '*la France profonde*' of the far South is concerned, they may well have not done so. The next exciting event for us was the arrival of the age of the motor-car, here some twenty years after Paris.

But it came. Not into the village of course – a *village perche* with slopes of 1 in 5 along narrow impassable *ruelles* is not ideal motoring ground. But somehow the village has adapted itself to necessity and hidden spaces have been constructed to accommodate the beast wherever possible. The French song-writer, Charles Trenet, who coincidentally died while we were murdering this masterpiece, wrote many songs about everyday events. One of them, called '*A la porte du garage*', seemed to fit the bill for the next episode.

In its first verse it depicts two bright young things meeting at the garage door and, in its last, the same two meeting in the same place 60 years later. So here was an opportunity for drama and pathos at the same time, an opportunity not missed by the church-warden, who had divested himself at last from his gorilla outfit, and Pierette, another generously endowed French lady of a certain age. Our choir certainly amply demonstrates the drastic improvement in living standards of the villagers over the centuries. .

'*Je t'attendrai a la porte du garage,* sang the choir, '*Tu paraitras dans ton superbe auto*' while Jean-Paul and Pierette appeared from the side of the stage posing as youthful automobilistes complete with helmet and gloves, and grew progressively older during the course of the song, Jean-Paul finally sporting a fine white beard reaching down to his ankles and a gnarled old walking stick. *'Ce refrain que les larmes aux yeux, ils repetaient au deux bons vieux'*. A fine example of growing old gracefully.

No chance of catastrophe here one might say unless he trips over his beard, but that would be to underestimate the Eus choir's ability to transform circumstance into catastrophe. The stage, a makeshift platform of wood resting on sturdy wooden benches was reached by a series of wooden staircases. It wasn't high, in fact not more than a few inches, but then my chorale is not young and needed help to reach it.

Nor was it large in area. To act at its front was to send those unfortunate enough to sing at the back of the choir spilling off into the void. Not only did this render the singing disjointed and variable as successive waves of chorists fell down the back, but their efforts to regain foothold meant that the choir was continually moving back and forth as in the ebb and flow of the tide. All of this took place behind Jean-Paul and Pierette while they were acting out their fantasies precariously near to the front of the stage.

By this time those in the audience who had not succumbed to sea-sickness were in fits of barely suppressed laughter, a fact recognised, but not understood, by the principal players. For sure, Trenet had written a light-hearted tune but not one calculated to have the listener in stitches. It must have been due to the brilliance of the acting, they thought. Finally the inevitable happened. Jean-Paul took one step too many in the wrong direction and fell backside over elbow into the audience, where those whom he had belaboured previously dressed as the *homme de tautavel* initiated their own personal war on terror, and took this unexpectedly early opportunity to wreak silent and satisfying revenge, in the pretence of helping a poor unfortunate to recover his dignity. As he limped off, helped by a confused Pierette, the audience continued to enter into the spirit of the performance by stamping their feet, honking and clapping their hands wildly.

Time passed yet again. We conveniently ignored two global conflicts, the rise of the aeroplane, the invention of the computer, the coming of unsalted butter and Golden Grahams, and ring pulls on beer cans, as insignificant items in the life of the village. The next item on the programme brought us to the present day with an acknowledgement of changing times, changing people, changing nationalities.

Firstly Marie the school-ma'am had written a witty little playlet in which a Dutch visitor with a Swedish wife in search of a Catalan house meets a raunchy French *vendeuse* who tries to seduce him. This is followed by the entry of a loud-mouthed Australian named, inevitably, Bruce complete with corked hat, leading a British Sheila who can't understand a word of the beautiful language, and a stuttering Spaniard who can't find his mule. Stereotypes all, but showing, for a small village in the middle of nowhere, a fine awareness of different national characteristics and customs.

But what an opening for expressive drama and what prodigious ham was on display in these *vignettes*. It was there by the hockful from every nationality, as if every amateur dramatic performance in every village hall throughout the continent had saved up it own porcine contribution to this moment in time. In places it was pure spam. Lacking a true Australian, the Brit who played Bruce gave the most godawful imitation of Strine ever heard outside of the Chipping Norton church hall on Anzac day. Had it been heard in the more remote parts of Queensland he wouldn't have survived for more than five minutes. '*Strewth, Sheila,*' he intonated, as the corks on his hat dangled dangerously near swallowing range, '*Get an eyeful of that mountain. Mount Kangaroo I think they call it*'

Sheila put on the plummiest faux-British accent imaginable in reply. Even 1940s BBC newscasters couldn't have matched it. And of course, through all of this, being in a foreign language, and a fairly impenetrable one at that, the audience was totally flummoxed, their faces registering complete bemusement at the antics of the *etrangers*. But they liked the hat, probably the first of its kind to reach these parts. And they must have loved the slapstick histrionics because they gave the actors, for want of a better description, a loud cheer at the end – or perhaps the shouts were the local equivalent of '*gerroff the stage.*'

The point of all this was to demonstrate that this is the age of Europe, a fact which even a small village in the Pyrennees cannot ignore, largely because people from other parts of the continent are the only ones who can afford to buy houses there. It is a wonder that this mini-invasion of the new barbarians is not more resented than it is. But by and large they don't, partly because those who do come here permanently are so lovable (I say this with a certain amount of bias), and more because they get themselves stuck enthusiastically into village life, including my choir.

There has been a worrying trend recently for an influx of what the brits call Essex man, anti-French, anti-Europe, anti-culture, demonstrating all the values of the dreaded British tabloids (we glimpsed our first copies of the Sun and the Daily Mail in the supermarket last year), but they are not yet enough to ruin the carefully-built reputation of the current batch of *etranger*s.

Consequently, to celebrate the arrival of a new political dynamic, we unearthed another Trenet song, *'Douce France'*. It extols the sweet virtues of life in France, a fact which most of us recognise, or else we would not be here. *'How sweet is France'* we sang in French, *'That dear country of my childhood. How I keep you in my heart.'* ' *My village, with its church-bells and proud houses, where children of my age shared my happiness.'* Such naked sentimentality brought tears to the eyes of audience and the French portion of the choir alike. The hall was almost awash with tender reminiscences. No thespian excesses for this one, just words of love. Sick bags were available for the Brits but not used.

But Marie had inserted a small amendment in the tail of the second verse. *'Yes we love you'* it read in most un-Trenetlike English, *'And we sometimes understand you. Good to be here, always watched by Canigou'* before reverting to another change to the original words in French, *'Douce France, pays de la tolérance, Nous t'offrons cette romance, Qui nous vient de notre coeur.'*

Well, you can't get a better welcome than that in a strange country. The offer of a heart felt romance in a spirit of tolerance is not one to be taken lightly in this day and age. There was just one slight hitch. The song had been choreographed to allow the *étrangers* to come to the front of the apron in order to sing their little piece of it. However, such is the volume of *étrangers* in my choir that their efforts to push forward in order to reach the limelight knocked a good proportion of the French singers off the stage at both sides and the front like tenpins in a strike.

It was something of a *désastre*, and affected the flow of the song considerably, not to mention the togetherness of the two protagonists. Here was 'l'Albion perfide' at its most typical. As the French clambered painfully back into view, I must say that the spirit of said *tolerance* was sorely tested, and the word was sung with gritted teeth by more than a few. But the audience didn't notice and nor did they care. For them this was part of the entertainment and they cheered the return of the natives with great enthusiasm and not a little sympathy.

We were coming to an end now. It remained only to sing Ludwig van's European hymn as a gesture of solidarity, and this we duly did in full throat and, I have to say proudly, mostly with the right notes in the right place at the right time – in all three verses! The Catalan, French and European flags flew reassuredly over us. It was a frisson-making experience for all, and one which surprised certain *etrangers* from across the channel, whose European commitment tends to be based more on what they can get out of it than what they can put in.

And so the show ended – in a treaclepot of European togetherness. But this is where there is a serious point to be made. And where my British bass (the immigrant) gets all philosophical and probably pompous as well. We, my choir and the audience, had a great time exploring the history of the village through the ages in song and dance. But we also learned something else along the way. It gave some of us an insight into what is different about this place from the places we have come from. Here history isn't to be found in books or in boring lessons at school. History is actually experienced by all of the people all of the time. History is what happens to our village and the people who live, and lived, here. It's connected - history is the present and the future as well as the past.

I know it's all words, but I think that we, villagers and *etrangers* alike, are all playing a part in the great cosmic scheme of things from the stone age, through the dark and middle ages and the excesses of the selfish 19th and 20th centuries, to the different imperatives of a 21st century and beyond. Even in our small village we have television bringing our nightly fix of murder, massacre and mayhem. And even in our tiny shut-off minds we can understand that peace and understanding between nations and peoples is the only way to solve most of the world outside's problems. And if this means more *détente* with our old enemies, and more *entente cordiale* with our even older enemies then so be it. And if that means building a new Europe and breaking down the outworn idea of nation states then so be it too. It's part of the connectedness of history, and our village knows all about that. We just proved it does.

I often wonder what the choir leader of 2100 will include in the programme. Will there even be a chorale at that time? Will there be a village? Will it contain any French people? I wonder if we at present in the village are leaving anything of value for those yet to come, just as those who lived in, and through, the past left something for us, never dreaming that 'us' would include a large smattering of people of other nationalities. Anyway, here endeth the sermon. I can only report that I can still hear the applause of the audience ringing through the rafters of the village hall. It was rapturous! And that, for me, makes it all worthwhile.

Please Note: the names of the principal actors have been changed to protect the allegedly innocent.

TALES OF THE CONFLENT

Chapter the Seventh: The Dog's Tayl

Being the story of how a dog bred to tend sheep transferred his vocation to human beings and became royal

The Dog's Tail

Hi! My name's Artur and they asked me to contribute my two pennyworth to this book and that's what I'm doing now. Whatever it may say elsewhere I'm the real owner of this place. I look after the other two humans and make sure they come to no harm. They also have a couple of cats but that's another story. I hate 'em and if I had my way they'd go within the hour, *toute suite*. I'm not averse to little ethnic cleansing and what I have in mind makes Iran look like a liberal democracy. For some reason or other they won't let me near 'em and keep shutting doors between me and them. I think somehow, thick as they are, they know what I'd do. Tarzan and Grimethorpe indeed - more like matt and mutt.

Anyway, as I was saying, this place is mine and nothing gets past it without me having a word or two to say about it. By nature I'm an easy-going sort of chap - well those damn sheep my ancestors used to look after make you that way - but don't think I'm going to let anyone know that. Not at least for the first ten minutes. Now if you're a female hooman I'll ease off straight away. Gorgeous creatures females and they always say the right things. 'Oh what a beautiful dog'. 'Quel beau chien', 'Magnifique' - words like that.

Very discerning animals are females and I like them. As for the other sort, well they're OK too but one's got to assert one's position in the pecking order hasn't one and after all they're all visitors into my house - except him! Him? I'm expected to call him master. I ask you, master! But just to humour my mistress I'll string along. Like I said I'm an easy-going sort of cove.

Oh he's alright in a peculiar sort of way. A bit head in the air. I don't think he liked dogs very much, but I soon sorted that out!. Always sitting in front of that stupid machine with the pictures and tapping away on those little buttons. Sometimes I wonder about his mentality. You know what I mean? No-one can be all there who just taps on buttons all day can they - asylums must be full of them. And when he's not doing that he's talking to himself into one of those brown plastic things. A bit rum he's allowed out in the world, if you ask me, but I suppose he's quite harmless and I let him think it's him who's protecting mistress, and not me. He says I'm beautiful too - which I suppose shows some traces of intelligence.

The two of them keep wittering on to the visitors about me being named after some king in olden days who was both British and French. Artur, I ask you - what a name for a dog of distinction - what's wrong with Rover or Fido or even Billy the Briard. They reckon that it had to begin with an A because I was born in 2006. What stupid rules these humans do dream up! Anyway, I'm secretly quite pleased. I could fall for this royalty business - didn't the guy have some knights who went around rescuing damsels in distress? Wouldn't mind doing a bit of that. Ah we're back to females again. That's a bit of a sore point with me. Now there's that Alsatian bitch in the farm across the way. Most of the time she's a drab and ordinary girl and we play together in the peach fields. But every now and then she must buy some perfume - and boy does she smell good.

Funny thing though, that's when her owners lock her up on their balcony - and my mistress starts to get all jumpy about my state of health, just because I don't eat as I usually do. That's another funny thing. I suppose - somehow my appetite goes on the blink and other things start to happen. It's at these times that all the scrubbers in the neighbourhood seem to turn up like bad pennies. Every tree in the peach field seems to have a scruffy dog hiding behind it. I see 'em off of course on my nightly preamble to the end of the lane, but somehow they're always back before I've reached the upstairs lounge. A real liberty I call it.

I remember once when I lived in England - I've been around you know, none of this sitting in the same field in all weathers looking after those bleating quadrupeds. To my knowledge I've lived in 50 different houses, though some of them they called by another word, hottles or something. Quite poky some of them were. And then there was that cage they put me in for 6 months, in case I was going to give them some disease or other. With lord and Lady Quarantine I think they called themselves, though what forty has to do with it I don't know. Forty days and nights of purgatory – and more? Forty times more horrible food? And horrible's the word. Anyone can tell by looking at my name and that funny inky thing in my groin that I have the blood of kings. And if they didn't believe that, they could have taken a sample of my royal blood.

Thank goodness for common sense they've started a new scheme that doesn't degrade us monarchs like that. Pet's passport or something. But they still squirt some repulsive stuff into the regal bottom when we go to that place where master and mistress were born – Bowlton I think they call it, though my bowl never seems to merit an increase in the biscuit field. And that's another liberty. If I had my way those bum-prickers would be straight off to the kennels on death row without a moment's hesitation.

But always remember it's me who paid the price. I'm the Martyr King who suffered so that the dogs of today can enjoy their freedom from Forty. Every now and then the old folks would come to visit me while I was doing the stretch. They looked so happy to see me and of course I was delirious to see them. Being shut up in a poky cage day after day is nobody's idea of fun - cruel I'd call it. Anyway, when they called time we were all mournful as hell so I used to get between them and the door and challenge them to take me with them. What else can a dog do to drop a large enough hint? Didn't happen of course. Humans are such strange animals.

Anyway, as I was saying before I so rudely interrupted myself - the memory of that still rankles - I remember once when I lived in England after that affair, I heard master saying to mistress that I would make a good stud. I'm not sure what that meant but since it was mentioned in the same breath as bitches my ears pricked up - well they're already pricked up on account of the fact that they were snipped and stuck together for 11 months so that I would look like a French Briard rather than an English one.

After all I'm French and proud of it - not xenophobic mind like a lot of English humans and French dogs I know, but proud. Anyway - why do I keep rambling like this? perhaps it's old age getting to me - he happened to mention that my grandfather was champion of Europe and my mother, bless her, was champion of Luxembourg. Well you can imagine how I puffed up at that. My relatives, champions. They didn't say champions at what but who cares. I expect that Luxembourg is another name for world.

Anyway, about this stud business. Apparently most British Briards, most British dogs they say, suffer from consanguinity - I think that means in-breeding because of the fact that they stuff all the best dogs in cages for 6 months like I was and people won't bring in new blood, so to speak. Well you can guess how excited I got at the prospect. Me, Artur, son of champions, king of kings, the most desirable dog in England, a fact I already knew of course, and all those bitches just waiting....... But apparently it was not to be. My mistress vetoed the idea on the spot. I don't know what came over her. It is the one other thing which rankles in my brain, but I try to shut it off except in my dreams.

So they asked me to give my views on the Conflent, so I shouldn't digress like that. For me it's the best place in the world - a bit hot at times because my wonderful body is covered in thick beige and black wool, but that's an insulator in hot weather as well as a protection against the cold. Every morning I take my mistress for a walk. In summer it's quite early because of the heat - about 8 am. But in winter they're lazy devils and sometimes it gets 9.30 before I can get him out onto the grass, and that can get quite embarrassing for me at times.

Anyway, after breakfast we jump into the car and she drives to a lake near a place called Vinca. I'd drive myself only I've never had lessons. Lovely spot. Apparently the humans use it as a beach in summer and windsurf on it. I could never understand why anyone would want to do either of those things. And they call themselves the dominant species? How can they say that? They fight and kill each other too! Now me and other dogs have our differences from time to time but we don't actually make weapons of mass destruction so we can zap other members of our own species into oblivion, including bitches and puppies. I reckon I've got more brains in my front paws than that lot put together. If I could only communicate everything I know, I know the world would be a much happier place.

Well, there I am running back and forth and generally doing things royal dogs do in such circumstances when up comes this pack of 3 depraved Alsatians and proceeds to attack me. I ask you - they must have been republicans wanting to establish a revolutionary council. I may be big and tough and able to look after myself but I can't fight 3 bruisers bigger than me so I lie down and make like I've submitted. But do they accept this and lay off? No they don't - it seems that they are determined to commit regicide. At this point enter mistress.

She screeches and flails her arms about and kicks the would be assassins until they retreat. She's a brave girl my mistress - she could have got horribly disfigured but I'm not sure that any living creature could have withstood banshee-wailing of that calibre. Anyway, along comes this bloke who says he's their owner and she starts on him too in a ripe mixture of French, English and words I thought she shouldn't know. I've never heard anything like it - normally she's such an agreeable person, but by the time she'd finished with him he was a pale creature. Mind you she had a point. The buggers could have and would have killed me - and it's supposed to be me whose protecting her!

That's happened only once and for the most part we both delight in our morning walks. She talks to me a lot, sometimes in baby language, which I resent. I'm an intelligent dog and a king to boot. My family are champions and it isn't necessary to address me as if I were a pea-brained idiot. But I guess neither of them know any better. When we get back home she puts me upstairs in the lounge on the balcony and closes the door. I think she knows what I would do to those cats if I could get near them. One of them has the cheek to come and stare at me through the glass - I'll have him yet. Mind you, it's nice being up on the balcony. The view's something else and I'd see most of it if it weren't for these damn cataracts and this hair in front of my face.

But those poor hunting dogs. Pup, am I glad I'm not one of them. I mean I sometimes think my mistress comes the old miser when she's handing out the winalot. But she's madame beneficence itself compared with the hunters. They starve the little sods to death till their ribs stick out sideways and they can sniff out a pimple on an elephant. Every Saturday, Sunday and Wednesday we're afraid to step outside the door in case we get bullet holes where they shouldn't be. Just read the hunter's tale in volume 2 to find out what a set of brittle-brained ignorant rednecks they are. I mean, I always thought I was a little macho, and, to be truthful, I believe that me and Genghis Khan would have been true soulmates.

In my *Weltanschauung* - big human word that - learned it from the old man. He's always talking about paranoia, globalisation and using big words where small ones will do- showing off if you ask me. Anyway to my way of looking at things, humans would exist only to supply pedigree pal on demand, cats wouldn't exist at all and bitches would -…..well, we won't go into that again just now. Where was I? Oh yes - compared with those babies I'm a pussy-cat - worse than that black animal I can never catch.

There they are, waiting in every ditch and layby, field armoury at the ready - I wouldn't be surprised if some of them have tactical nuclear missiles - and blazing away at every creature that dares to breathe. They're supposed to put up 'keep off the hunt' signs but half of them can't be bothered. You're walking happy as Fido with a bone round a corner, and suddenly you find a gun barrel pointing up your left nostril with intent to maim.

Mistress goes scatty at the mention of hunters - says they've no right to ruin our morning walks and if she had her way, she'd be hunting them. And I can't say I don't agree. She's used a ripe choice of language at some of them - words I didn't think an elegant lady like her should have known. No way you'll find us out in the countryside between August and February. We're liable to get blown to animal heaven with the sangliers and the izards. Still, there's one statistical consolation - more hunters shoot other hunters than seem to shoot the things they think they're meant to be shooting at.

Seems to me to contain a little poetic justice there. And for what? I mean you don't find us dogs spreading such death and destruction all over the countryside. Must be something in the human psyche that drags the race down to that level. When it's seen itself to its logical conclusion and every human's destroyed every other human and most other species as well, then will be the time for the Briard race to put some dignity into living on this planet. Except for cats, of course! They're doomed.

They've done the lounge up well, I have to say. It covers the whole of the area of the house and, one time, they had more than 60 people in it listening to that music scraping away at one of their interminable concerts. I can't say I enjoy those - the music's too loud for my delicate royal ears and one note's very much like another. After all there are only seven notes from a to g and there's a limit to what anyone can do with those.

Anyway, as I was saying, half of the lounge is tiles and it's lovely and cool in the summer. I spend hours lying there developing my 'principia philosophia canina.' If only I could find a means of conveying the secrets of life to my fellow canines, some of them might not behave like raving lunatics every time someone comes to the house. Mind you I do too. After all I'm billed as a *chien de garde* and my picture appears on the post box downstairs looking fierce.

I can't say I like that picture - it shows just that little too much tongue and my beard needed a teensy bit more attention than it got, but it will do to keep some of the less desirable intruders away, and the bark does the rest. I'm rather proud of that bark. It is deep and profound in every sense of the word. It resonates and puts the fear of death into anyone, with or without malicious intent, especially that pesky feline. But I know the difference and behave accordingly.

The old folks - I hope they don't mind me calling them that, but they are really old and sometimes they often behave that way - have friends who visit often and they all like to sing at the tops of their voices while they are eating. Sometimes there's as many as 16 of them yodelling in the kitchen where the tiles make it sound like they're all inside a toilet. Me, I'm under the table half dying of shame and half-deaf with the noise of it all. If only my ears would close - perhaps the British Briards have some advantages after all.

Anyway, afterwards they all troop upstairs and I follow, tongue hanging out pretending to be the faithful ally, and they start once more. By this time they seem to have gone gaga, laughing helplessly at the most inane of jokes - never a one about the dog who crossed the road or the identity of that bitch I saw you with last night. Perhaps it all has something to do with that liquid they're forever pouring down themselves - they never give me any - or it could be the clothes they nearly wear. Anyway I put on my 'we are not amused' look and retire to the corner as far away as I can get.

I know some of those people well by now. There's the couple who think, quite rightly, that I'm wonderful and are always digging their fingers into the wool round my neck. I think it gives them some kind of a thrill. I like them and thought they had good taste until we paid a visit to their house and I saw they had a white cat. You'd have expected something better from a bloke who's got Dr in front of his name. Perhaps it means Dogs refused. Then there's the guy who claims he hates dogs. I've got him sussed. I catch him looking at me out of the corner of his eye and I know that he's big softie really.

His wife's a sweetie and I expect she keeps him on a leash. If only he'd open up his heart to me like she does. Another two sometimes bring their big daft spotted dog. Nice feller, but thick as two bones in a ditch. If he'd only stop his tail beating the shit out of everything in sight, I'd try to get closer to him to see what he thinks of my principia philosophia canina for dogs. There are two other humans who would understand it I am sure. They seem to permanently inhabit the vague world of philosophy, but I'm not sure about their capacity to make the higher conceptual leap for understanding canine postulates.

From time to time my master and mistress go back to England, where they have those repugnant cages. Several people offer to look after me but they don't think anyone could cope. They're probably right. So I am driven down to kennels at the other side of Perpignan. They try to console me with such dumb platitudes as ' Whose going on his holidays then' or ' Lots of friends where you're going Artur'. It's pathetic! They're just saying it to salve their own conscience.

But I don't mind too much because the lady down there is one of the few humans who can recognise canine genius. I remember when they came to collect me the first time. 'Ah', she said 'Artur, 'qu'il est sage, qu'il est beau, qu'il est superbe'. Wise, handsome and brilliant - she has me described to a t. What a woman! Ever since then I've been trying to share with her my new ideas for a principia canina mathematica for dogs, but somehow she keeps butting off to see to other, less intellectual, animals. Perhaps it is just that she's able to recognise a prodigy but can't understand the celestial nature of its being.

When I take my mistress shopping - she says she takes me, but who's she trying to kid? - I lie in the back of the car discouraging the odd burglar or car-thief. It's a mundane task for a royal dog to perform, but it gets me out of the house and off the street corners. The three of us occasionally go for long rides into the countryside. It's extremely beautiful round here but the roads on these trips are very twisty. I have to confess that my attention span suffers considerably by having to hang on for grim life while master hurls the car round the corners.

That's another thing about him. Since he's come down here he's started to drive like the Catalan suicide squads who sometimes try to come and join me in the back of the car. Add to that I get just a tiny bit car-sick - never actually have spewed, but I've been very close. I groan convincingly occasionally and mistress gives him a sharp word, but after a few kilometres the guy's a goner. Nothing's going to shake him out of his little dream until he's shaking the bottle of champagne at the end of the journey.

Another thing I hate besides those 4-legged horrors are those yappy little motor-bikes. They seem to hand them out to the youngsters with their coco pops nowadays. They go round wearing those take-me-to-your-leader helmets and revving up the engines until the royal ears hurt. They're worse than the singing. Every time one comes up behind the car I always get into an artificial paddy and show them exactly what I think about them. If they're overtaking - it only happens when mistress is driving, correction, it *always* happens when mistress is driving - I wait until the psychological moment as they pass my window and give them the full 100 decibel bark.

You should see their faces. Even with that painted goldfish bowl on their heads they get the full impact just at the crucial time. One or two of the less experienced ones nearly fall off. Trouble is, it frightens the people in the car as well - even I am impressed by the sheer power of my voice, I think I should have joined a dog opera - and they give me some welly. Is there any justice in this world? Here I am trying to protect them from the incipient encroachment and deleterious consequences of noise pollution - I must remember to include that down in the principia - and they give me the old rough language.

Anyway, I got my own back on that guy who goes past the house - the one who doesn't like humans never mind dogs. Real old misanthrope. There he was coming down on his noisy old phut-phut and, joy of joys, with a pair of step-ladders under his arm so he couldn't defend himself. Mistress had left the front door open so I bounded out, wool waving, in my usual effervescent style towards the feller. You should have seen him swerve - I wasn't going to touch him mind, I know better than that - he nearly ended up in the ditch. I'll give him this though, he didn't actually fall off. But oh my the trouble it caused.

Was I in the Briard-house for that? The old man was away at the time, in a place they call Japan I think - I've read that there are some sweet borzoi bitches over there - and mistress had to go out and apologise. But was he going to accept any old apology from a woman? Oh no, he was not. He insisted on talking to the old man and threatened to have me put down. Can you believe it. A regal dog like me. The guy has no perception. Anyway when the old man came back he smoothed it over, and I got a reprieve and a formal reprimand. The door hasn't been left open since - but just give me one more opportunity and I'll finish the job. He puts the fear of Dog into mistress.

Did you ever notice how dog is an anagram of god. I've been thinking a lot about that lately and I'm sure it isn't accidental. I'm beginning to wonder if I'm more than royal if you catch my meaning. After all didn't all sorts of supernatural things happen when the other Artur was around? And people keep saying that my mistress worships me. Well, it does make you think. I know she goes down on her knees a lot when she's brushing my coat, but I hadn't put two and two together until just now, though why she has to torture me during her devotions I really don't know. Perhaps it's a sort of self-flagellation carried over to me. That's

one thing will definitely go in the principia canina, the philosophia
I think rather than the mathematica, though perhaps I should start
a principia canina diviniensis for dogs, simple to let them know
about their spiritual heritage.

Every now and then we have some of those young human
visitors. Some of them can scarcely totter. My Dog, do I love them.
They're even less able to communicate than me, and so very
impressionable at that age! This is where I can really do some
influencing and bring them up on the fundamentals of the
principia. So, using all my considerable skills of wit, charm and
overwhelming personality expressed through wagging my tail, I
go right up to them and start the mesmerising. I'm bigger than
them you see and they are so sweet. The gentle light of love is in
my eyes if they could but see them. But there's one thing I really
can't understand. Here I am trying to give them the best of starts
in life and all they can do is start screaming for their parents, as if
I were a bug-eyed monster. Can't they grasp the subtleties of
body language, or is it my divinity they can't cope with?

Anyway, mistress tries to explain that it's in my nature to love
children - dead right on that score, mistress - and that I simply
want them to play with me. Play my paw, this is a serious
business of education and I cannot comprehend why I am kept
apart from the little blighters for the rest of their visit. It's such an
opportunity lost for them. At these times the logistics of the
household get quite complex. I have to be kept apart from both
the cats and the children, so doors open and close like it's a
Whitehall farce.

I expect to see Brian Rix coming down the drive in tennis shorts
on a rickety old bicycle any minute. The more I think of it the
more I am sure that it's my god-like nature which puts the humans
off. They can't cope with it you see. They have to believe that they
are the only beings on this earth with free will, the power of
reason and in-built divinity. What utter nonsense. Since when has
human been an anagram of god?

And there's another thing that gripes me from time to time. When
mistress and me come back from our little morning tête-à-têtes in
the countryside, what does she give me? A slap-up meal like King

Arthur used to get. Not even close – a bone that's what! I ask you! A bloody bone for a dog of the first estate! It's an insult to my station in life. And it's not even a real bone from one of those animals that must have had an accident – hopefully a cat. No way - it's one of those cow hide things that smells like an elephant's bum. At least it's what I think an elephant's backside would pong like if I had any idea of elephant cuisine. I get this information about other creatures from the telly, you see.

The two humanoids are always putting on nature programmes – to show how spiffingly educated they are I suppose, or to pay penance for eating animals. Anyway, they think I'm not paying attention just because I've got my eyes half-closed. But I notice, and that's how I know about elephants. And I know a lot of other things they think I don't know – like what human beings get up to when they've had a lot to drink. They think I don't notice all that fumbling about, but I do. However, to return to the touchy subject of bones, I go into the garden and bury the stinking things. Whereupon they fall about in great ecstasies of delight as if it's the sort of things dogs do for any other purpose than getting rid of the stench. Human beings? They seem to have the collective intelligence of a plastic cat. Dog knows what gets into their plebeian little heads. I don't and I'm a King.

I've been thinking a lot about that recently – well, they never taught me to read so there's an abundance of contemplation time. Since I am the first estate I ought to have subjects and a kingdom. No-one has told me who these might be or what the territory will entail. So, in my mind, I've been re-arranging the hierarchical furniture so to speak. Well, there won't be a normal second estate will there. I mean dogs aren't normally religious and I've never heard of a canine archbishop. But I'm going to write it all down in the principia canina governensis when I've learned how. My mistress will be the Arch-bishop, Lady Chancellor, Prime Minister, Lord High Executioner, my right hand factotum and keeper of the tin opener.

She can delegate the job of actually opening the tins of Royal Pedigree Pal to the lesser orders. I'm not sure what job I'll give to him. In my new world order I'm the master and he's almost unemployable. He certainly can't be trusted with the tin opener.

Maybe he can be keeper of the harem – and everyone knows what has to happen to the candidate before that post is filled. There will of course be a large number of perfumed bitches in it. I heard somewhere – on the telly again I suppose – that the last Chinese Emperor had 3400 concubines, as I think they called them. He even had a Palace built to house them. Well now, if that means what I think it might mean I'm going to have more than 5000 of them, they will comprise the second estate and I'll have a huge dog edifice built to house them.

I might call it the Forbidden Kennel. They will be the only ones allowed to vote and they will only be allowed to vote for me, if they know what is good for them. Sounds a little dictatorial I suppose but I can't be bothered to set up a press and television system that will do it more subtly for me, like most of these so-called liberal democracies do. The third estate will be all the dogs, humans and other beasts in that order of importance. Tress will be obligatory at all street corners and at every 10 metre interval between. All cats will be exiled to Antarctica.

Anyway, enough of dreams, I'm supposed to be extolling the virtues of the Conflent, and the only connection I can think of is that it's a divine place to be. The food's a bit unambitious mind. Quite apart from the bones, tins of Pedigree Pal and wholemeal biscuits meal after meal don't exactly sound like the nectar of the Gods, but it's surprising how the old salivation glands start to motor come feed-time. I often go to meals with the old folks. I don't actually enter the restaurant mind.

The last time they tried that someone brought a Golden Setter bitch to the table across the room and the next thing was that the two tables were almost together. I enjoyed that, because she looked as though the principia canina mathematica would have been just up her street, but it has rather kiboshed the idea of effecting entry to other restaurants. When they come out and start discussing what they've eaten on the way home I sometimes wonder if I'm missing out on something, but some of the foodstuffs they mention sound disgusting. I mean what on earth is *Caille a l'Oignon*? And who the hell would want to eat little birds anyway?

I often hear my ancestors complaining - I have this acute race memory, you know - that the humans used to put them out to look after the sheep and lambs, and be blowed if they didn't then go and eat the very animals we were supposed to be protecting. Might as well have left them to the wolves. Very strange creatures human beings, and arrogant with it! Never mind. Perhaps one day they'll see the light, master and mistress will invite the neighbourhood and we'll all sit down to a nourishing meal of Pedigree Pal. That should make them sing!

Really, that's all I can contribute about the Conflent. I can thoroughly recommend it to all the dogs who want to come down here. The tree population is quite exquisite. But look out if you're an English dog, it takes six months to get back into your own home if you haven't taken precautions, and I don't recommend the waiting period. I'm even thinking of an idea for my next contribution to animal happiness. It's called principia of dogging around the Conflent. Maybe I'll publish it some day. I'd sign off by saying wuff, wuff, ruff, ruff. - but wouldn't that just be too corny?

I hope you all have a super time in the Conflent, just as I do, and don't forget to look me up - especially if you're a bitch wearing that haunting perfume......

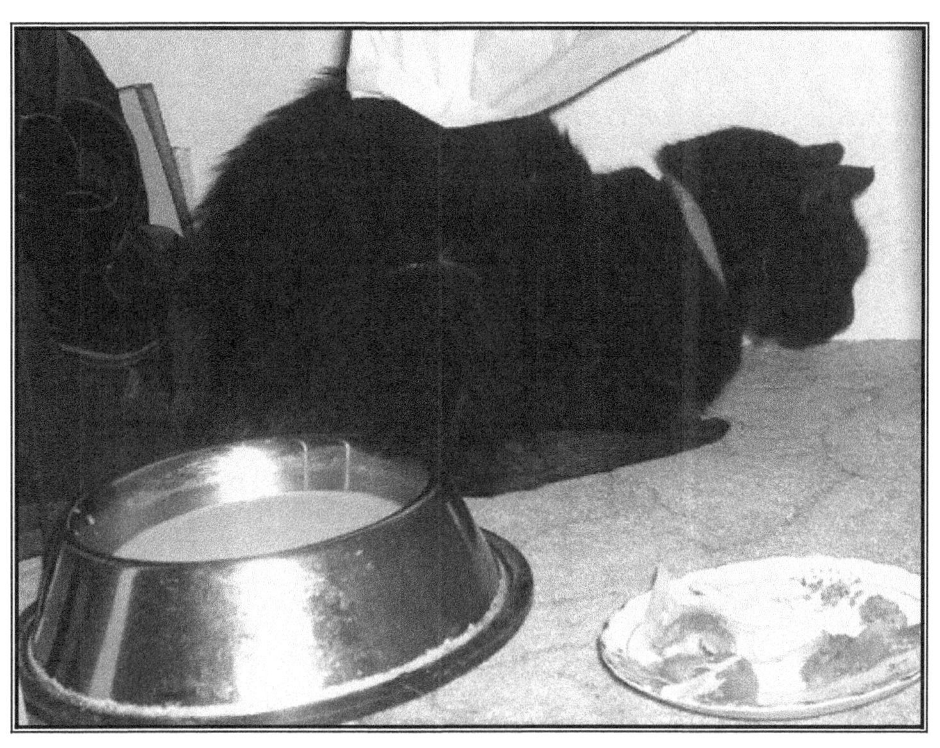

THE CONFLENT TALES

Chapter the Eyghth:

Grymethorpe's Tayl

The full unexpurgated details of how Tibbles challenged the dog, the world and everything, and won

My name's Grimethorpe. They asked me to say a few words about living in the Conflent. Some disparaging remarks were made about me in the last chapter and I'd like to start by putting the record straight. After all, that barking lunatic from upstairs has had his chance. Now it's my turn to make a few points. Personally, I can't understand the guy. He gets his three square meals a day just like me - why the hell does he want to make a meal of me as well. He's a raving nutter. You can tell by the way he nearly bites his own tongue off as soon as he sets eyes on a member of the feline race. At first I took it quite calmly, hoping to show him by example how to behave in a mature and responsible way. Some hope! A totally useless strategy, like the dog himself.

I remember that one time mistress forgot to shut the upstairs door. The bugger was down in a flash, breathing fire and brimstone. Well, I showed some coolness and dignity I can tell you. I sat there on the chair just giving him a look of utter contempt. I do contempt brilliantly, just like all the things I do. Did that stop him? Like feline life on Pluto it did! I could almost feel the hot breath of death, when mistress suddenly discovered her mistake and started wailing like a deranged harridan.

That made him pause for just a second and that was enough for Grimethorpe, né Tibbles. I was off like a leopard with diarrhoea. I'd rather be a live Grimethorpe than a brave ex-Grimethorpe, contempt or not. Ever since then objection has been the better part of value. I doubt you'll get the paw-shake that starts any kind of peace process in this household - he's a dangerous psychotic and should be locked up in a prison for good with the key thrown away.

Psychologically I should be more of a mess than him. Well, it isn't surprising is it, given my family background and the traumas of my early life. Mother wasn't exactly the most careful of lovers. When she was in the mood, she never thought to ask her partner whether he was equipped with the wherewithal or if he'd ever had the two bricks treatment. Nor was family planning in her feline vocabulary. Consequently every 6 months or so along came another ready-made fox meal. In my case it was a 4 course feast for the beast. Only I was lucky. I used my feline nouse and hid round the corner keeping quiet - not easy when scared witless. This went on for a few weeks and what was mother doing at the time? - and father too, whoever he was? - keeping well out of the way that's what.

Then I saw these 2 bipeds arrive in the car and bounded out to greet them with my most pathetic bleat. You should have seen their faces. In the first place they were surprised, but that soon turned to soppiness, especially the female one, and I knew I was in for a ball. A few more pathetic bleats for good measure and there I was in front of a saucer of milk. Within the hour they'd dashed off to the supermarket and bought some kitten food. Heaven had arrived, and not before time.

Anyway this blissful life lasted for about 4 weeks - they always ate out on the terrace and while they were eating I always played around their feet just to remind them I was still here and not forget to carelessly let drop a few tasty morsels. Then, one day, I heard them say they were going to leave and go back to some country they called England, wherever that is. Well, the old knees started to tremble again, I can tell you. Back to the status of foxmeat in a single sentence. Don't these bipeds ever understand the consequences of their actions?

Then they started talking about who else would look after me. Looking for a soft touch, if you ask me, but I wasn't going to complain about that. I like soft touches. Anyway the upshot is that they invited my present master and mistress for dinner one night and she gooed like a deranged cow at me the whole evening. I liked that - it represented hope. Him -he wasn't impressed at all. 'We've got to have him' she said. 'No bleeding way' he replied, the hard-hearted bastard, 'The dog would go mad'.

I'll give him this he wasn't wrong there. Except that, now that I've met the animal, I'm sure the canine oaf was mad already. As for me, well this was my continuing existence they were discussing and I couldn't care less if they had a grizzly bear in the house. So I put on my most pathetic bleat and that sealed it - we had a deal. She gets to put me in a basket and transports me to salvation and he gets to call me names.

Now I'd grown use to Tibbles. If it can't be Pussy or Felix, then Tibbles seems to me a reasonable compromise. So what does the old sod come up with? Grimethorpe! that's what. He said something about it being after a brass band in a mining village somewhere in a place called Yorkshire because he happened to be listening to it when I arrived in the box-like thing. But I know he just did it to spite me. I suppose if he'd been listening to the weather forecast instead, I'd have been called Rockall or Malinhead. Sometimes I wonder about the sensitivity of these male human beings. Some of them show as much humanity as the Sphinx - and we know what happens to *him* at the height of certain seasons.

And *she*'s not much better - she's shortened it to Grimy! How would you like to be outside playing with your friends when your mother comes to the door shouting 'Grimy' - meaning yours truly? Hardly likely to enhance personal dignity and self-esteem, let alone the respect of your mates. Makes a cat feel inferior. I know I'm a black cat, but I spend a lot of time with the old tongue trying to wash it all off. And there isn't a speck of grime anywhere on my sable torso.

Don't think I haven't heard the stories about black cats - we hear things we felines you know. I've heard that in England they regard it as lucky for me to cross their path. What I'd pay to get there! I'd even spend 6 months in those damn cages that frothing animal upstairs talks about to get there. I'm good at crossing paths too when the mood takes me. Here in France it's seen as unlucky. You should see those stupid French humans scuttle as soon as they see me, and that's before I had even contemplated crossing their path. What self-respecting cat would want to do that, anyway?

All except him and her. Well him, he's never with us if you see what I mean. Always thinking about something else - how to save the world, how to develop half-witted strategies for some stupid thing he calls Lifelong Learning, how to think up asinine names for us cats. Like most egg-head professors he's a bit absent-minded. Did I say a bit? Sometimes, it would take a posse of trained sheriffs and deputies with indian trackers to find his mind. He writes books.

I ask you, what sort of a cissy, fatuous occupation is that? Forever sitting in front of that square shining thing and pressing buttons. It's not as if I, or any cat I know, can read or understand them - and I hear, no names no packdrill you understand - that the human beings can't understand them either. Still, it can't be as bad as the principia drivel that deranged four-legged lunatic upstairs comes out with.

As for her, she suffers from an overdose of something she calls tlc - stand for two loopy cats, she says. I suppose that's her little joke, but it does speak volumes about the mentality of the master race - or in her case the mistress race - doesn't it?   Anyway, when she comes banging the food tin, I give them both the disdainful treatment. I'm not after all a slavering dog like that gruesome quadruped upstairs. I only give in to reason when I can't wait to eat any longer.

They've built this hole in the door with the flap that goes in and out. It's supposed to offer entrance and egress - Do you like that word? I saw it on the package when they opened it. But it must have some kind of locking mechanism because sometimes I can't open it no matter how hard I push. More than once I've been fleeing like a porker with piles from that gang of vicious females across the way and hurled myself through the hole only to find that the inside of the house didn't appear like it ought to have done. Instead there's this crunching noise as my face hits the plastic and a permanent headache for a week afterwards - not to mention the squashed nose. I expect the bleeding females would have had me too, if they hadn't been screwed up in the road laughing their tiny stripes off.

But my mistress isn't all bad, which is more than I can say about him and that crazy bat-eared moron upstairs. At least she cares. And, if push comes to shove, I'm a bit fond of her. Well, she makes sure the old bowl's topped up with the whiskas at the crucial time and fills up the water butt so Grimethorpe can top up with the liquid gold. I like to reward those who show me kindness and every now and then I bring her presents. They're in the nature of an educational course in the wild-life of the region.

But I'm not sure that she's grateful. She *says* thank-you every time I bring a live mouse in for her to play with as a reward. But you can tell can't you, by the inflection in their voices, that sometimes they're less than pleased. I think it's because these humans are so damn slow. As soon as I let go of the thing, instead of leaping after it and stunning it with a single blow of her paw, she let's out this an almighty yell and gives the poor sod a heart attack.

Then instead of popping it into the pot for the next hearty meal for the family, she sweeps it up and puts it out of sight in the dustbin. I just can't fathom these people out. Once she even opened the door and let it outside again, and before I could point out her mistake and retrieve the vermin she closes the door in my face. I ask you, what sort of expression of gratitude is that? I think these bipeds have double standards - I hear them moaning about the mice and how they want rid of them, and as soon as I do my heroic bit, they complain about my methods.

It was the same when I gave them a mole and a dormouse as a present. Thank-you Grimethorpe, then shock horror, you just killed the tiny furry thing that's digging up your garden, eating the roots of your plants and in general creating mayhem under the lawn. You'd have thought they'd be jumping over the moon about that, but they sure as hell don't show their gratitude in any tangible way like extra whiskas or a place at the table while they're eating that delicious roast chicken.

Then there's the lizards - mostly little ones and incredibly fast - almost as fast as me. But I get the bleeders in the end - in more than one sense. I wait until they think I'm not there, then I strike. Most of them escape but not before I've got a piece out of their tails. I heard mistress say to master once that she thought we had a peculiar strain of tail-less lizard in this area and should they report it to the wild-life people.

If only they knew. If only I could tell them. In fact if the latter were true there are a lot of things I'd tell them - like how to get rid off that felicidal maniac upstairs. I get around the property a lot and I can tell you I know a lot more than they can about the woods outside the house. For a start, there are some other funny looking animals with stripes on their head - badgers I think the humans call them. Seems to me they all go around calling each other Bill. They seem civil enough and I always get a polite nod when they pass me by. But they're a bit stand-offish and haven't invited me in to their living room for tea yet.

The farmers round here certainly don't like them. Mention the word badger and they're out with their gas-guns without so much as a gentle tear. That's when Grimethorpe gets to be elsewhere, gas-guns not being in my line of activity. And there's always the chance in the heat of the moment that they might mistake a black cat for a stripy badger. Mind you, mistress gets quite soppy about them. She says they're a protected species - seems to me that's much more than I am - and the farmers shouldn't be doing what they are doing.

But then the farmers round here are a law unto themselves. Weed-killers are supposed to be banned, but I've seen them spreading it about on the grass like it was chocolate coating. Tastes horrible and makes me fart, but that brainless nincompoop upstairs seems to think it's the next best thing after friskies. There are compensations. I'm always pleased to see him groan away with a bad stomach afterwards, though not with the odour. .

Every now and then mistress puts me into one of those baskets shaped like a piece of late twentieth century art, and bundles me off to the vet. It's usually just a prick to stop me getting a nasty bout of rabies or whatever, but last time I went they did something drastically different. Thank goodness they put me out with an injection for that one! I suppose it's better than two bricks, but it still isn't right, is it. Well it makes a mockery of a chap. The female cats across the way haven't stopped laughing since I came back much the worse for wear and without the equipment to make an impression.

Every time I go out to protect my territory, they're over the other side of the road making high-pitched noises and mincing their walk. One of them, the mother, is a really vicious bruiser. She gets her claws out and gives me a good scratching. Of course I fight back, but three against one isn't good odds. One of them's going to kill me one of these days - if that degenerate fiend upstairs doesn't get me first. Twice I've had to revisit the vet while he drained the septic stuff out - pus from puss if you see what I mean, and that's the only joke I'm going to make because I'm not into humour - not even black humour - oops there I've done it again.

You'd have thought that *they* would have protected me. What a hope! I don't expect anything from that tongue-wagging idiot upstairs but at least the humans might raise a finger. It's three o clock in the morning and there I am outside wailing like an air raid siren just to warn them that the territory's under attack. Do they dash out of the house with the meat cleaver or a bucket of water to see off the attackers? Do they even man the barricades in the bedroom to repel boarders? Not a chance! The rest is silence. So who has to stand up to the three witches from Hell? Lucky old Grimethorpe, that's who. So they look at the battle scars the next morning and tut tut about the depraved nature of next door's cats. I could have told them about that, and did! They didn't turn a finger when it really mattered. As soon as they get in the bedroom they seem to go deaf as a weasel with attention deficit syndrome.

Mind you the operation didn't affect the old voice-box. It still gives out a fine baritone rendering of the cat's cradle song and the pussy-love song from Mimi - better than any other feline *chansonnier* I have heard. And it's certainly not the counter-tenor it could have degenerated into. Even the malicious matrons across the way are impressed by its subtly smooth cadences and the warm delicacy of its lower registers.

It makes those nightingales in the wood sound like a three-chord rock group. Many is the time I have serenaded the waiting world with the ethereal, and timelessly cultured arias of a forgotten paradise, only to be rudely halted in full voice. It can only be jealousy, or perhaps they are simply tone-deaf. Beautiful music of the sort I produce should be recorded for posterity, but instead of the tape-recorder they bring pails of water and shout rude words. That fatuous hellhound from upstairs starts to bark in competition - but who could possibly believe that that monotonal yapping could match the ineffable majesty of a maestro like myself in resonant vocal throat?

As far as the musical talents of humans are concerned I tend to agree with the slavering idiot - it must be the only thing we agree on. They are indescribably bad. A cross between Andrew Lloyd Webber on an off day and Harrison Birtwhistle on a good one. They are so limited. They don't seem to have any more than 12 tones to play with. Nowhere near the 42 tonal significances, the 30 chordal characteristics and the 10 register attributes through which we cats can express the entire feline range of emotional musical poetry.

I've heard them here in our kitchen and it's enough to put one off whiskas for life. How these limited beings can call themselves the planetary rulers I cannot begin to understand. And master - he thinks he has a fine baritone voice too and boy does he use it, especially when he's had more than a couple of drinks. Then the rest of them join in, homerwauling like that notorious Eus Chorale. That's the time to say a temporary goodbye and retire to the wood to look for the Bills. At least they have more musical sense - that is the sense to know that they can't sing, and so don't try to.

I have heard – it is only hearsay mind – that up in the village there's a whole army of cats of the stray variety. Living in the great outdoors with none of these stone constructions they lock us up in at night. I'm told that a female human goes up there every morning and night and leaves food for them all. Not exactly Whiskas you understand but good wholesome bread and scraps of meat. Think I might check that one out one day. Sounds idyllic to me – no brainless nincompoops like that one upstairs to avoid, no belligerent shrews to snicker at me, no doors that suddenly turn solid. All those lovely feline companions to sing to all night long.

Here it's like living in darkest Ruritania with only the bills to say hello to. The more I think about it the more attractive it seems. But then what about the foxes? What happens when that icy cold white stuff comes down and freezes my bits off – that is if I had any. What would they think about me not having any? Can the human be trusted to come with the goods every day? OK then, maybe I'm better off here where at least the food is guaranteed, the radiators are warm and there's a bed for me to sleep in.

But I'm no intellectual. That raving imbecile upstairs thinks he knows a thing or two. Principia philosophia for dogs indeed. Royal blood, baloney. Divine tendencies my furry ears. I've heard him talking to his mates, but more often than not he talks to himself. After all who'd want to socialise with a disreputable lowlife like that? He's just living in a fantasy land of his own making. You wouldn't catch me philosophising or thinking profound thoughts. In fact, come to think of it, you wouldn't ever catch me thinking at all. Just not up my alley. Personally, I doubt I've had a decent creative thought in my entire life, and why should I? I'm just an old reactionary. I reckon if I lived in England I'd be a Sun reader, or even worse the Mail. I'd rather believe all that self-righteous drivel than think for myself.

And now I have another cross to bear. Another bleeding cat to share the premises and pinch my precious stocks of whiskas. Tarzan - I ask you - what sort of a name is that. The little sod could no more swing through the trees than I can ride master's bike. And then you get that woman from down the road, what's her name? -

Saying 'you Tarzan, me Jane' and sniggering away like it's the greatest joke ever told. It's no wonder these humans have psychiatrists. They're all shot through with hangups about this and torments about that - full of angst and guilt-ridden as rubber ducks at migration time. I hear they beat their young - what sort of depraved behaviour is that, I ask you?. One day someone's going to lock them all in a big room together with their depraved canines and throw away the key. Me - I couldn't care less. The only thing is - who's going to open the tins of whiskas?

Anyway that's my contribution to the Conflent awareness campaign. I don't get around much, and when I do they put me in a cage. But if there are any cats out there reading this, my only advice is to avoid this place like the plague. The musical life comprises just me and a few voles with squeaky voices. The social life is practically nil, and what there is is hostile, full of potential terrorists. In addition there are vicious brutes everywhere out to get you - especially if you're black. But then I hear that's true in other places too.

I think I'll just curl up in this nice warm bed by the radiator and think thoughts of what might have been. Maybe life here isn't so bad after all.

Just one last blow of the trumpet. If you enjoyed reading this book, you will also enjoy the other 'Conflent Tales' book called, not surprisingly, the Conflent Tales Volume 2 .There you will experience the joys of feasting in the 'Mayor's Tale', the pleasures of the dance in the Scottish Country Dancer's Tale (in France of course where it has become a whole new art-form), the charm of the Culture President's Tale, the hunter's and the wild boar's tales and many others. But of course the book will have woven its magic when you actually come to visit this most beautiful part of the earth's surface.

If you have been inspired by the beautiful poetry shown in parts of this book, you may be interested in his other poetry books, all of them available from Amazon for both kindle and as a paperback. They are

Poems for a Learning Nation

Poems for a Safer Planet

Albert (kindle only)

www.ingramcontent.com/pod-product-compliance
Lightning Source LLC
Chambersburg PA
CBHW072225150726
48002CB00005B/1947